10 WEEK BIBLE

2 SAMUEL

10 Week Books
10WeekBooks.com

2 SAMUEL: A 10 WEEK BIBLE STUDY

Scriptures taken from the Holy Bible, New International Version®, NIV®. Copyright © 1973, 1978, 1984, 2011 by Biblica, Inc.™ Used by permission of Zondervan. All rights reserved worldwide. www.zondervan.com   The "NIV" and "New International Version" are trademarks registered in the United States Patent and Trademark Office by Biblica, Inc.™

ISBN: 0-9997312-0-3
ISBN-13: 978-0-9997312-0-8

Cover: David hands the letter to Uriah, Pieter Lastman 1619

10WeekBooks.com

For Emily

Your smile has always been infectious. From the first day your mother and I laid eyes on you, we haven't stopped smiling ourselves. I pray that the Lord would give you a deep love for His Word and that forever you would be fascinated by Him.

CONTENTS

ABOUT THE 10 WEEK BIBLE STUDY

My heart is to see people fall in love with God through growing in His Word. The 10 Week Bible Study helps people do that through repetition, helpful commentary and engaging questions. Most of all, this study helps people stay engaged by encouraging them to keep going when they get off track, get confused or get lost.

David, in Psalm 1, told us that if we meditated on God's Word day and night, we would be like a tree planted by rivers of living water. I don't know about you, but I find it hard to remember to meditate at all hours of the day. The 10 Week Bible Study makes that easy by encouraging people to read the book of the Bible being studied 10 times in 10 weeks (hence the name).

When you start reading God's Word like that, you'll find that you accidentally meditate on His Word. In those moments when your mind is at rest and blank, it always snaps to something you've been thinking about. When you pull up to the stoplight, maybe your mind goes to work, chores or that show you've been binging on Netflix lately. With the 10 Week Bible Study, you'll find yourself thinking about God's Word in those moments. You may just catch yourself asking God questions about what you've been reading without even thinking about it.

That is what David meant by meditating on God's Word day and night, that your heart and mind are so full of His Word that you can't help but think about it in those quiet times.

ADDITIONAL RESOURCES

Join the growing community of people who listen, watch and discuss the 10 Week Bible Study online. With millions of downloads and thousands of free resources to choose from, the 10 Week Bible Study produces daily podcasts, videos and other downloadable content to help you grow in your walk with God.

For more information and to join our email list to get regular encouragement in God's Word, visit 10WeekBible.com today.

INTRODUCTION TO
2 SAMUEL

2nd Samuel is the continuation of the story started in 1st Samuel. Both books were actually written as one and separated into two books for length in modern Bibles, so we are actually picking up our author's story halfway through.

Speaking of author, we don't actually know who wrote the book of Samuel. Even though it bears his name, Samuel died years before the completion of the story in the book. Many scholars believe that Samuel wrote or compiled many of the stories from his lifetime and that the prophets Nathan and Gad compiled the stories that complete the book.

2nd Samuel details the reign of David as king, focused on his conquests of other nations and trouble through two civil wars and rebellion. Unlike many biographies, David's is one that very clearly outlines his greatest strengths and most glaring deficiencies. We gain a clearer picture of the man that God called "a man after my own heart."

OUTLINE OF 2 SAMUEL

2 SAMUEL IN 10 WEEKS

2 SAMUEL 1-2

STUDY QUESTIONS

1. How did Saul die? How do we know?

2. Why did David kill the Amalekite?

3. Why would David write a lament for Saul? Could you have done the same thing for someone who spent years trying to kill you?

4. How do you think David knew the Lord told him to choose Hebron for his capitol?

5. Why did David thank the men of Jabesh Gilead for burying Saul?

6. What do you think was the point of having twelve men fight each other in front of the two armies?

7. Why did Abner tell Asahel that if he killed him, he couldn't look Joab in the face?

COMMENTARY NOTES

2 SAMUEL CHAPTER 1

Samuel is really one book in the Jewish Canon of
scripture. Splitting it into two books is purely logisti-
cal because it makes for a more consumable narrative.
We pick up the storyline at an opportune season as
Saul has just passed away in battle with the Philistines
and now David is set to assume his rightful place on
the throne of Israel.

SAUL IS DEAD
1:1-16

David had just finished chasing down a large group
of Amalekite raiders who had taken all his stuff, wives
and children as well as everything of all his men.
David hit possibly the lowest point of his life when his
men talked of killing him because of their great loss.

David convinced them all to chase the Amalekites
instead of killing him and they were able to catch
them and recover everything they lost and more, but
it was in this context that we enter the story here at
the beginning of 2 Samuel.

Thinking he was bringing David good news, a man
came to tell him of the story of Saul's death. This man
obviously had not heard of the events of David's recent
past, because if he had he would have known that
David didn't want any news, good or bad, from an

Amalekite. The man told David the events we have already heard of atop Mount Gilboa but with one twist. Instead of falling on his own sword, the Amalekite tells David that he graciously killed Saul himself when he was asked.

Many people forget that 1st and 2nd Samuel are one book split into two and misunderstand the two narratives we are told about Saul's death. They see these two stories in conflict and assume that the authors did not know which was true, but nothing could be further from the truth. The author of Samuel here wants us to know that the truth is that Saul fell on his own sword as we are told in 1 Samuel. That is the narrative that our author relays to us, but this new narrative is told through the mouth of this young Amalekite, thinking he will receive a reward for killing David's adversary and stripping him of his crown and band.

David, still fresh in his anger against Amalekites, and devastated by the news of his in-laws and beloved friend Jonathan's deaths, gives the order to reward the Amalekite with the same reward he claimed to have given Saul.

Even though David knew he was the rightful king of Israel, he never wavered from the fact that Saul was still very much the anointed current king of Israel, and that no one but God Himself had the right to take that away from him. David took that anointing as a very sacred privilege and responsibility before the Lord. No one on earth had more reason to want Saul dead, but David honored God's choices and plans far above his own.

At this point, the only version of the story David had heard was the one the Amalekite presented, so David believed it and had the young man put to death for his treason. One wonders if the young man quickly began recanting of his story as the execution order was given.

DAVID'S SONG FOR SAUL AND JONATHAN
1:17-27

As David was lamenting Saul and Jonathan's passing, he wrote a song to commemorate them. He would go on to make it compulsory learning for everyone in Judah after he became king. We also discover here that the song was written in the book of Jasher, one of the source-texts many scholars believe Samuel was compiled from (this is not the same book of Jasher that some people read today).

"How the mighty have fallen" is an unforgettable statement to make of the man who tried to kill you repeatedly. David found himself in a continually awkward position because of Saul, but his trust in God for his position and supply gave him great grace for his adversary.

David sings of how he longs for the news of Saul's death not to be boasted about by the Philistines. Remember that at the time of this story, David was living amongst the Philistines. What a tumultuous world David lived in!

Not only does David show his reverence for Saul through his lament for he and Jonathan, but he actually curses the ground on which they were killed. David praised Saul and Jonathan for their exploits in battle; something not just important for bragging rights. Before Saul, Israel was constantly bombarded on all sides by raiding bands. There was a constant threat of everything you owned and loved being taken and killed by your foreign neighbor, and Saul brought that to an end for a large portion of Israel.

Not only did Saul bring a relative peace to Israel she had not previously known, he also brought prosperity. They normally go hand in hand, but David praised Saul for clothing the daughters of Israel in "scarlet and finery," a reference not only to gifts Saul likely made but also to the prosperity in the country to afford such luxuries.

David concludes his lament by weeping for Jonathan. Here he proclaims that the love and affection for Jonathan was greater than any love he had experienced for a woman. This is not a sexual reference to Jonathan, but a comparison that how he felt for him far surpassed that kind of love. Remember the kindred spirit that David and Jonathan shared: Jonathan attacked an army of Philistines like the Israelites had never seen before all by himself and David took them on by killing their giant champion. Both were cut from the same cloth and they realized that kindred spirit.

David ends his lament with the phrase, "The weapons of war have perished." This may sound offensive to many Westerners today, but in David's day this was a serious problem. We tend to allegorize many biblical events today like "fighting our own giants," equating David's battle with Goliath to facing conflict with coworkers. We do this because we do not have literal nine foot tall murderers threatening to give our carcasses to the buzzards. Most of us do not live under the constant threat of someone showing up one after-noon to kill us and take all our stuff and daughters to be their sex slaves. With Saul dead, Israel had lost her general and defender.

So much fear set in when Saul died that almost all of the Israelites fled their land and retreated to the east side of the Jordan river. War for David and his people was not a bloodsport to pass the time; it was survival itself.

2 SAMUEL CHAPTER 2

DAVID ESTABLISHES HEBRON AS CAPITOL
2:1-7

Our author does not tell us how much time passed between David receiving the news of Saul's death and moving from Philistia back to Judah, but we can probably assume it was between weeks and a few months, but not years. The important part of these first few verses are not that David moved to Judah, but the fact that he asked the Lord if he should and where to go.

Saul only inquired of the Lord when he was in dis-tress; David made a habit of seeking the Lord for even the smallest decisions. The Lord was gracious to answer David that He had chosen Hebron for him to reside in for now. Hebron was God's choice, not David's. It was a home for David and his fledgeling kingdom to reside during the conflict that would ensue for the next several years.

The leaders of the people of Judah came to Hebron and anointed David king over them. This was a significant and joyous occasion, but it would certainly be seen as an act of sedition by the rest of the nation. When a monarchy is established, it is through that family line that rulership will pass. David had no right to the throne by blood. All Israel knew now of David being anointed by Samuel, but he had been long dead and David had been living in Philistia. Any prophetic right to the throne paled in comparison to what seemed more logical at the time. Saul had one remaining son who eleven tribes still saw as their rightful king.

David learned a lot about politics during his time in Saul's army and then while running from him. Encounters with the other generals, including Abner, and with people like Nabal, David began to understand how to garner the favor of people and how to push them away. He employed some of that political charm in dealing with the brave men of Jabesh. He honored them for their treatment of Saul and Jonathan's bodies and then tried to leverage their clout within Israel to convince them to follow Judah's suit in anointing him as king. Unfortunately for David, they weren't yet willing to follow him.

First Contact
2:8-17

Early on, Jonathan had been acting captain of Saul's army, but because of his impetuous nature or due to perceived inability, Saul put Abner in charge. Abner was Saul's uncle. Still in the family, but not as close as Jonathan, Saul probably felt he could control Abner more than his very independent son.

As a relative to the royal family, Abner probably could have made an attempt at the throne himself, but he seemed to be more honorable than that and actually took the authority and prominence he himself had and used it to establish Ish-Bosheth as king. Ish-Bosheth would prove to be a poor commander-in-chief and almost a puppet king behind Israel's true leadership under Abner.

There are many questions left unanswered by our author here. The timelines laid out do not quite match up as we would expect them to, and we are never told how Israel retook all her homeland back from the Philistines. Abner anointed Ish-Bosheth king in Mahanaim, on the east side of the Jordan, so they were obviously still in some transition years later.

Our author tells us that Ish-Bosheth was king for two years, but that David ruled in Hebron for seven and a half years. Does that mean that David established himself as king over five years before Abner anointed his cousin as king? What happened to the northern kingdom of Israel during that time? It seems possible that for five years Israel had remained leaderless and somewhat in exile east of the Jordan, but the details of those five years are almost completely absent.

Based on the stories of David's mighty men in this book and in Chronicles, it would seem that to some extent David was fighting Israel's battles and pushing back the Philistines from their land while Abner and Ish-Bosheth were in exile. After some time, Abner took the army back to Gibeon to try and reclaim from David what he felt belonged to his family. Joab, the commander of Judah's armies and David's nephew, heard of Abner's presence and went to meet him in Gibeon.

At first, the confrontation seemed amicable. There wasn't open battle when the two armies met; there was conversation. These were all men who to some extent knew each other. We will see that Abner was familiar with Joab, Abishai and Asahel. It is possible that they had followed David to join the army after his encounter with Goliath and had served under Abner.

Abner called out to Joab and suggested a one-on-one battle between the best of each of their men, a competition of sorts. It might have been that Abner wanted to see just how skilled David's men were at battle. Maybe Abner thought he could show off the skill and strength of his men and dissuade Joab from continuing any aggression.

We do not know if the twenty-four men all faced off simultaneously or two-by-two, but the results were the same. Each man was crafty and evenly-matched so that not one of them survived. Instead of being the

11

competition Abner had hoped for, the combat turned even bloodier than it began. Joab and his men got up and chased Abner.

CIVIL WAR
2:18-32

In full retreat, Abner and all his men ran as quickly as they could away from Joab and David's men. As they ran, Joab's men slaughtered them. In those days, generals led from the front and were often the most accomplished and fiercest warriors, superior in skill and physique. Abner proved himself to be quite the physical specimen as he was able to run away from Asahel, thought to be one of the fastest men in David's army.

Not only could Abner match Asahel's speed, he was also able to carry on a conversation with him as they ran. Asahel was determined to make a name for himself and kill Abner, who he knew was Israel's true leader, and bring the civil war to an end. Though he was quick, Abner knew that Asahel could not match his ability to fight.

Abner begged Asahel to take out his aggression on someone else whom he was more evenly-matched with, but Asahel refused to listen. Instead of facing off, Abner surprised Asahel and just stopped abruptly and jabbed the dull end of his spear into Asahel, his momentum helping the spear to run him through. The details here are gory, but war then, and now, is nothing but gore. One day the atrocities of human arro-

gance and evil will be replaced with the perfect rulership of God Himself and war will cease. Until then,
the unnatural breaking and dismembering of human
bodies for the sake of the betterment of a few select
men will continue.

It seems that Joab did not know Abner had killed his
brother when he ended the conflict with a word of
peace that day. Joab's anger burned so hot against Abner for revenge afterwards, that it seems unlikely he
knew until they returned to bury their dead that he
learned of his brother's bloody passing.

Abner returned to his place of exile on the east side
of the Jordan in Mahanaim and Joab returned to Hebron the next day to bury his brother. Both armies
marched all night to get home, a testimony of how
miserable this civil war was going to be going forward.

War is hell, as William Tecumseh Sherman put it,
and instead of unifying around the common cause of
ridding their land of Philistine oppression, David was
now forced to fight two wars. He and his men continued to fight the Philistines but they also dealt with
continual aggression from Abner and Ish-Bosheth's
men. They may have seen him as their rightful ruler,
but it was David who was returning Israel's land back
to them while Ish-Bosheth hid in cowardice far away
and did nothing to help his fellow countrymen.

Don't forget to read 2 Samuel this week!
Visit 10WeekBible.com for more resources including daily
podcasts, videos and more.

2 SAMUEL 3-5

STUDY QUESTIONS

1. Why did Ish-Bosheth accuse Abner? Do you think it was true?

2. Why did Joab kill Abner? Why didn't David have him killed for the murder?

3. Why did David have Ish-Bosheth's assassins put to death? Weren't they at war?

4. Why did Israel wait for the death of Ish-Bosheth to make David their king?

5. When David made Jerusalem his capitol, he had been king 7 years. Ish-Bosheth was only king for 2 years. What do you think happened during the other 5 years?

6. Why would the king of Tyre send cedar and masons and carpenters to David?

7. Why do you think the Philistines attacked David when he became king instead of sending gifts like the other nations?

COMMENTARY NOTES

2 SAMUEL CHAPTER 3

CIVIL WAR, CONTINUED...
3:1

The chapter and verse breakdowns were not part of the original texts of scripture, but were added within the last thousand years for the purposes of making more accurate reference to passages of scripture. The men who established the commonly held chapter and verse distinctions today had their reasons for where they split things, but we can certainly take issue with them today. Verse one, even though it seems transitional, belongs in chapter 2.

Ish-Bosheth and Abner could not maintain what little power and control they had over the other eleven tribes of Israel as David continued to fight for and regain control of the land of Israel from the Philistines. We know that David was fighting these battles on behalf of Israel because of stories like those found in 2 Samuel 23. As David retook Israel back from the Philistines, he looked more and more appealing to the Israelites than Ish-Bosheth did.

Ish-Bosheth is a case study in fighting for the wrong things. Instead of retaking the land from the Philistines like David was, Ish-Bosheth was only concerned with keeping David from leading the people. How often do we encounter people the same way today, fighting the wrong battles? Instead of working together against common enemies, people are constantly mired down in competition against one another. What would the church in America look like if she stopped trying to compete with others and instead worked together at fighting against the work of the devil in peoples' lives?

DAVID'S SONS
3:2-5

David began having children in Hebron, and in this passage we are told their names. We will become more familiar with all these names as we progress through this book, but one name stands out. Absalom is the grandson of Talmai king of Geshur. When royal families joined together in marriage in ancient times it was almost always the seal of a treaty.

Handing over a daughter in marriage to a nearby king is a great way to ensure peace because it becomes harder to attack that kingdom when your grandchildren live there now. David probably made this pact with Talmai as a means of securing the entire land of Israel. He now had Ish-Bosheth in a pincer position between himself in the south and Geshur in the north. Strategically, it was a brilliant move. In the case of the peace of his family, maybe not so much…

THE NATION UNIFIED
3:6-21

When Saul died, all his belongings, taxes and

17

palaces were bequeathed to Ish-Bosheth. That meant taking care of his father's concubines, those women who were either part of the royal harem or were married to the king but not of aristocratic standing. Rizpah happened to be an important part of Saul's harem as we will see throughout 2 Samuel.

It was common in those days to try and steal away the wives of principal leaders and kings to shore up one's own position. After all, if a man could steal that which is most precious to another man, how much more could he do for a nation? To take another man's wife, especially the wife of a fallen king, would mean that she had chosen him as a successor as someone close to the previous king.

These are the devious actions that many a war have been born of. Helen of Troy was taken by Paris, an act that led to the famous sacking of Troy by the Greeks. Mythical or not, taking another man's wife will always stir up trouble. We do not know if Abner actually did sleep with Rizpah, but there are some good signs that he did and in fact was guilty of exactly what Ish-Bosheth was accusing him of.

When accused, Abner did not deny that he had slept with Rizpah. Instead, he appealed to his loyalty to Ish-Bosheth's part of the family. It seems the resultant conversation was probably always part of Abner's plan. He may have been ready to steal away the heart of Israel with Rizpah in tow and turn it over to king David in whole. Ish-Bosheth's accusation only made Abner's resolve to do it more sure and quick.

Whether or not Abner had actually slept with Rizpah, the result was the same. He was tired of Ish-Bosheth's lack of action. He was tired of his weak leadership and he was tired of serving a man who only cared about keeping David out of power. When Abner lashed out at him, our author tells us that Ish-Bosheth did not respond at all because he was afraid of him. In doing so, we see who was really in charge of Israel all along.

Abner sent word to David of his intentions and David's only request was that he come with Michal, his first wife and daughter of Saul. He knew she was taking refuge with Ish-Bosheth in the East. Instead of leaving it up to Abner, David actually sent messengers directly to Ish-Bosheth demanding Michal be returned to him. Michal may possibly be one of the saddest women in scripture. Her father was not especially gracious to her, she was left by her first husband and ripped away from her second husband who obviously love her, and if that were not enough, we will see later that she will be unloved and childless.

Ish-Bosheth by now had realized that his kingdom was over so he immediately made plans to honor David's request. Maybe he thought that if he responded quickly David would let him live in exile as he had. David probably had no intentions of killing him because of his oath to Saul, but he wasn't long for this world either way.

Before crossing the Jordan, Abner consulted with all the leading men of Israel and unified them in heart and mind to make David king over all Israel. In doing so, he quotes a prophetic promise from God that we do not have recorded elsewhere about God using David to free the Israelites from the Philistines and all their enemies.

They are subtly mentioned, but when you start to assemble all the prophetic promises that David received through the years, we begin to realize just how patient he was in waiting on the Lord to fulfill His promises. Just imagine being promised as many times as David was that you will rule only to have people continually come against you, literally trying to kill you. Great promises from God are rarely birthed without great pain and struggle.

When Abner arrived in Hebron, David honored him. David knew Abner personally from his time under his command. During the feast, David and Abner probably discussed the particulars of how they would unify the kingdom and Abner left to go assemble the nation for David's coronation. Knowing his history with Abner and his relative contempt for Joab, David may have had it in mind to make Abner the new commander of the military. That fact was not lost on Joab.

ABNER MURDERED
3:22-30

Joab had been out on a routine raid against the Philistines when he and his men returned to Jerusalem and were told about the feast with Abner. Joab's anger flared up at David for allowing him to come and go in peace. His desire to avenge his brother's death would prove to be greater than his loyalty to David or his love for his country.

Joab sent messengers to catch up to Abner, presumably telling hm that Joab wanted to meet with him as well to discuss the coming unification of the armies. Abner had no idea of what was coming. He met Joab in an inner room, completely off guard. His conscience was clear about Asahel, and he had no idea of Joab's fury. Under false pretenses, Joab stabbed Abner in cold blood.

Joab's rage blinded him to what was about to happen. In one moment of hatred fulfilled, Joab had crushed the hopes of the nation of unifying. If it were not for other events out of all of their control, Joab would have indefinitely extended the civil war Israel was embroiled in.

When David heard about what Joab had done, he was furious beyond imagination. He cursed his nephew, his entire family and his future generations. Though Joab deserved to die for this premeditated murder in cold blood, David could not bring himself to exact true justice for the sake of his sister, Zeruiah. For now, David's harsh words would have to suffice as punishment against Joab.

DAVID'S LAMENT FOR ABNER
3:31-39

David forced Joab and all the army to tear their clothes to mourn for Abner. Joab had murdered him because of his desire for revenge and possibly because of his jealousy of a superior commander.

David made Abner's funeral a big deal. He himself walked behind the funeral cart and let everyone see him weeping for Israel's great general. It may very well have been because of Abner that Saul was never able to catch up to David during all the years he was on the run. David's lament was genuine, but he wanted everyone in Israel to see it, too. He wanted everyone to know that it was Joab and Joab alone who had Abner killed.

Our author tells us that David's political prowess was not lost on the people of Israel. He convinced them that he was innocent and in a moment of national tragedy David turned things around and made them all love him even more.

2 SAMUEL CHAPTER 4

ISH-BOSHETH'S DEATH
4:1-12

Our author takes a brief moment to explain that Jonathan had a young son that David did not yet know about. He was born to Jonathan during David's years of fleeing and he had been crippled as his caretaker fell on him as he fled from the Philistines. This is a detail that does not fit in the current narrative and may have been added later as context for Mephibosheth's upcoming storyline. It may have seemed to fit best here in the description of his uncle's death.

As we turn back to the main narrative of the chapter, we see who was truly in charge of the nation of Israel. Upon hearing of Abner's death, Ish-Bosheth was afraid. A good king would have been irate and ready for blood. Ish-Bosheth was a political coward.

Two of Abner's commanders under him decided they had had enough with Ish-Bosheth. In ancient days, a military loss by a king or commander was a national embarrassment, often paid for with blood. These two commanders decided they would make good on Abner's promise of giving the kingdom to David, so they murdered their king and beheaded him. They then rushed Ish-Bosheth's severed head to David in Hebron to receive their reward.

Rekab and Baanah had heard of the prophecies of David becoming king, but they obviously knew nothing of David's oath to Saul and Jonathan to protect their family after he had become king. David lectured them about the time the Amalekite came with the news of Saul's death and then proclaimed the same sentence over the two of them.

David's anger burned against Rekab and Baanah so much that he desecrated their bodies and hung them on display over the bathing pool in Hebron. He essentially temporarily cut off the city's supply of fresh water, forcing everyone to think twice before drawing water as their decomposing bodies rotted above the pool. This seems less like a political gesture and more like David's total disgust at how things were going for those who had been loyal to Saul.

For the time being, this act would show Israel that

David had no intention of seeing anyone else in Saul's family dead.

2 SAMUEL CHAPTER 5

DAVID'S CORONATION
5:1-5

We start chapter five with another prophetic promise not specifically given to us before. The elders of the tribes of Israel told David that they knew God promised him he would shepherd Israel and rule over them. They also acknowledged that he was the one who led Israel in their campaigns while Saul was king.

Even though Abner was officially Israel's general, David had quickly made a name for himself after the defeat of Goliath by continually striking the Philistines down at every turn. 1 Samuel told us that the people of Israel sang songs to commemorate how awesome David was.

By the time David was thirty it feels like he had already lived four lifetimes. At least he had seen enough trouble and experienced the joys and rejections and pains of four lifetimes. But when much is given, much is required, and that requirement often comes with significant testing. David's time of testing and preparation were now over and the Lord had made good on all His promises to make David king. The tests of a newly crowned king were far from over, however.

DAVID TAKES JEBUS
5:6-12

Always the shrewd political operator, David knew that ruling from Hebron might not be the best plan moving forward. He had an idea to move the capitol of Israel to a more neutral location than within his own tribe, so he selected a site within Benjamin. This was a significant sign to Israel that he was the entire nation's king and not just loyal to Judah. By taking up residence in the tribe of his former rival, David showed all the elders his commitment to the entire nation.

Jebus was a city that the Israelites had never been able to conquer. The city had a strategic geographic advantage with its steep hills. The walls the Jebusites built did not have to be very large to protect such a mountain, so they had never been unseated from their perch since the time that Joshua and Caleb led the Israelites across the Jordan River.

1 Chronicles 11:6 tells us that David had demoted Joab as commander of the armies of Israel because of his murder of Abner, because David offered the position to whoever was willing to sneak into Jebus and conquer it. When David made the open-ended audition for a new commander, he must not have counted on Joab's insatiable hunger for authority.

Although not specifically referenced in scripture, Jewish history tells us that Joab had to enter Jebus through a cistern or well with smooth walls and somehow scale an unscalable shaft to enter the city and sneak around to open the gates. Because David had made his offer in public, he was not going to recant even though Joab was the one to win the position of commander. In all, Joab would lose and regain his position three times throughout his life because David could never bring himself to do what was necessary with Joab because of his sister.

The old city of Jebus became known as Jerusalem, the "City of Peace." What is referred to as the City of David was mostly the original stronghold of Jebus with some expansion. Jerusalem in the Roman period and today is much, much larger.

DAVID'S GROWING FAMILY
5:13-16

David continued to expand his family through new wives and concubines. Although the Old Testament never tells us not to engage in polygamy, common sense and every recorded case of polygamy tell us that it isn't a great idea. It caused nothing but pain and trouble as anyone today could expect.

The names of the sons born to David in Jerusalem include two important names: Solomon and David. The lineages of Joseph and Mary can be traced back to these two sons of David as presented in Matthew and Luke.

DAVID'S CORONATION
5:17-25

David had been driving the Philistines out of Israeli territory for some time, but when they heard he had been crowned king, they decided it was the time to mount a new counterassault. The former allies went to war and were no match for David and his men. But the most amazing part of this story is not David's military acumen, but his ear to the Lord.

Again and again David would inquire of the Lord before launching out into a new campaign. David did not ask God to bless the campaign he was setting out on, but he would actually ask God's opinion about whether or not he should set out at all. How often do we fail to simply ask the Lord his opinion about the things we are considering? How often do we fail to ask God His thoughts on our lives?

Twice the Philistines attacked and twice the Lord answered David clearly. in fact, in the second attack the Lord provided a supernatural deliverance that surely convinced the Philistines not to attack David again. The next time David and the Philistines would meet, it would be on David's terms and he had his eye set on a little place he used to hang his hat: Gath and Ziklag.

Don't forget to read 2 Samuel this week!
Visit 10WeekBible.com for more resources including daily podcasts, videos and more.

2 SAMUEL 6-8

STUDY QUESTIONS

1. Why did David want to bring the ark to Jerusalem?

2. Why didn't David have the ark carried as the Lord had required?

3. Was it okay for David to be angry at God? Do you think it's okay to tell the Lord you're angry at Him?

4. Why do you think David wanted to make a temple for the Lord?

5. Why do you think the Lord promised David a descendent on the throne forever just for wanting to build a temple?

6. Why do you think David asked God to keep the promise He had just made?

7. Why do you think David was so brutal to the Moabites?

8. Why did the Lord give David victory everywhere he went?

COMMENTARY NOTES

2 SAMUEL CHAPTER 6

THE LORD STRIKES OUT
6:1-11

We are not told all the details, but at some point David understood that Jerusalem was the place where God had chosen to place His name in Israel.

You are not to do as we do here today, everyone doing as they see fit, since you have not yet reached the resting place and the inheritance the Lord your God is giving you. But you will cross the Jordan and settle in the land the Lord your God is giving you as an inheritance, and he will give you rest from all your enemies around you so that you will live in safety. Then to the place the Lord your God will choose as a dwelling for his Name—there you are to bring everything I command you: your burnt offerings and sacrifices, your tithes and special gifts, and all the choice possessions you have vowed to the Lord. And there rejoice before the Lord your God— you, your sons and daughters, your male and female servants, and the Levites from your towns who have no allotment or inheritance of their own. Be careful not to sacrifice your burnt offerings anywhere you please. Offer them only at the place the Lord will choose in one of your tribes, and there observe everything I command you.

Deuteronomy 12:8-14

How David understood that Jerusalem was that place we may never know this side of eternity, but because of what will happen in the coming years, it is obvious that David knew this clearly. Because of this, David understood that it was time to bring the ark of the Covenant into Jerusalem, so he prepared one of the grandest events in human history.

The ark was currently in Kiriath Jearim, only a few miles from Jerusalem. The path the ark had to take was very mountainous and difficult, so David prepared what he thought was a good idea to move the ark: a new cart.

The ark had moved several times in the past hundred years, but none of its movements were quite as well-known as when it was stolen and then returned by the Philistines. Near the beginning of 1 Samuel we are told that the ark caused so many problems for the Philistines, they decided to send it back.

"Now then, get a new cart ready, with two cows that have calved and have never been yoked. Hitch the cows to the cart, but take their calves away and pen them up. Take the ark of the Lord and put it on the cart, and in a chest beside it put the gold objects you are sending back to him as a guilt offering. Send it on its way, but keep watching it. If it goes up to its own territory, toward Beth Shemesh, then the Lord has brought this great disaster on us. But if it does not, then

we will know that it was not his hand that struck us but that it happened to us by chance."

So they did this. They took two such cows and hitched them to the cart and penned up their calves. They placed the ark of the Lord on the cart and along with it the chest containing the gold rats and the models of the tumors. Then the cows went straight up toward Beth Shemesh, keeping on the road and lowing all the way; they did not turn to the right or to the left. The rulers of the Philistines followed them as far as the border of Beth Shemesh.

1 Samuel 6:7-12

Unfortunately for David, this cart idea was not the Lord's idea. He had a much different version of how the ark should be handled, but the miraculous story of how it had been returned to Israel was what had stuck in David's mind. David's cart was probably beautiful. It may have been the most beautiful cart anyone had ever seen before, but the Lord didn't want the ark placed on a cart to move it.

Of all the places along the way that the oxen could have stumbled, a threshing floor seems like the least likely. There were several mountains and valleys between Kiriath Jearim and Jerusalem, but threshing floors were generally very flat places atop hills. The fact that the oxen stumbled on the one flat place on the journey speaks more to the Lord making a point than to a random accident.

When Uzzah touched the ark, he died instantly. That may seem like a harsh punishment for a man who was only trying to keep Israel's most precious treasure from being damaged, but the ark was so much more than that.

The ark was not a talisman of good luck. It was not an idol to be worshipped. It was an earthly representation of a God who was to have no image made of Him. The ark was the Lord's, not the Israelites'. When Uzzah reached out to steady the ark, it was as if he was offering the Lord some assistance. This holy box was never to be touched, the reason it had rings and long poles as described in Exodus.

Bezalel made the ark of acacia wood—two and a half cubits long, a cubit and a half wide, and a cubit and a half high. He overlaid it with pure gold, both inside and out, and made a gold molding around it. He cast four gold rings for it and fastened them to its four feet, with two rings on one side and two rings on the other. Then he made poles of acacia wood and overlaid them with gold. And he inserted the poles into the rings on the sides of the ark to carry it.

Exodus 37:1-5

This made David very angry. He had spent a considerable fortune on this extravaganza and had brought the entire nation together to be a part of it. To have it abruptly end like this was terribly embarrassing and it made David mad. This was a lesson to David that he would never forget, but we can also learn a lesson from David here, too.

As in many of his Psalms, David expressed his anger to God. Many times we feel like we cannot tell God we are angry, especially at Him, so instead we bottle it up inside or we tell others. There is nothing worse that we can do than that. If our hearts are reverent, we can express any emotion to the Lord we feel. In an understanding of the humility of his earthly position, there was no emotion or thought David tried to hide from God, because he knew he couldn't hide them anyway. It is far better to wrestle with God in our emotions than to hide them from Him and try to deal with them ourselves.

David's anger quickly turned to fear, so he left the ark there in the care of a man named Obed-Edom. As Solomon would one day point out, fearing the Lord is the very beginning of wisdom, for it is He, not us, who holds our lives and eternal fate in His hands (Proverbs 9:10). That fear is what causes us to initially come to God with reverence in full knowledge of our position before Him. Prostrate before God is where we learn how good, kind and loving He is, but we would never find ourselves in the position to learn from the Lord if it were not for that fear that first instructed us.

THE ARK FINDS ITS HOME
6:12-23

We are told in the Chronicles account that David sternly warned everyone that they must study and understand what the Lord had said about how to treat the ark the next time they attempted to move it because of the previous fiasco. But instead of quietly moving the ark into Jerusalem to save face, he doubled down and threw an even bigger party.

David was far less concerned with his own image before the people of Israel than he was with honoring the Lord, so he decided to bring the ark into Jerusalem once more. The sacrifices, food and fanfare of this event would only be eclipsed when his son Solomon would dedicate the temple a generation later.

On such an occasion, it would be normal for a king to build a reviewing stand in a prominent place in the city to watch the procession in great dignity. That isn't what David did at all. Instead of sitting on a perch high above everyone else to oversee his magnificent parade, David took off his kingly robes and put on the clothes of a priest. Not only that, David walked with the ark and all the common people, dancing.

There was something very special about this moment to David that caused him to put all his might into dancing. His great joy could have only come as a result of some revelation of what God was doing in establishing Jerusalem as that holy place where His name would rest forever. David had the distinct privilege of establishing the place where God would one day come and touch earth to rule and reign forever, and he understood the magnitude of this moment.

Poor Michal, however, could not see the magnitude of what was taking place. She only knew that she was not sitting in a reviewing stand looking dignified before the nation. If we've followed her story, we may want to give her a pass for being a wet blanket this day, but David's joy quickly turned to anger and he decided then and there that he had had enough with her.

David explained himself before Michal that day and gave us a window into his understanding of himself. He cared nothing for his own dignity or honor, but only for the Lord. He knew that if he had any dignity and honor, it only came from the Lord in the beginning, so he would do everything in his power to earn dignity from Him, not from the people of Israel, and he knew that in doing so he would earn their respect as well.

Our author here does not say that Michal was barren, but that she had no children all her years. Let the reader understand that Michal was probably not actually barren, but had no man to provide children for her from this point forward. What a tragic ending for a woman who had been through so much and suffered so much. She had never dealt with or overcome her pain and it caused her to miss one of the most significant moments in Israel's history, even the history of the world, something David would never forgive her for.

2 SAMUEL CHAPTER 7

THE DAVIDIC COVENANT
7:1-17

After David had brought the ark into Jerusalem, he set up a tent for it. This tent was special, because it was not the tabernacle. He left the tabernacle outside Jerusalem and people were still required to go there to make their sacrifices. David did something special with the ark during his time as king in Jerusalem: he set up a tent for it and let everyone come by and see the ark. In fact, David paid for singers and musicians to stand before the ark and sing and pray twenty-four hours a day, seven days a week hereafter.

After some time it occurred to David that he was living in better accommodations than the ark was and he intended to do something about it. Always wanting the Lord's opinion about his plans, David told Nathan the prophet of his plans to build God a temple to house the ark. David wasn't just telling Nathan in passing, he wanted to know the word of the Lord about his plans. But without asking the Lord's opinion himself, Nathan was thrilled and gave David the green light to do whatever was in his heart.

It wasn't until that night that the Lord spoke to Nathan in a dream or a vision that David was not to build a temple. Through his prophetic declaration, Nathan told David that the Lord was pleased with him and would establish his kingdom forever through his lineage, something that is not lost on us today. That kingly lineage would descend down directly to Jesus to fulfill this promise. In honor of this prophecy, Jesus will sit enthroned as ruler of Jerusalem forever, the Holy City that God intends to dwell with us in for all eternity.

But God did not want David to build Him a temple. David had been a man of war and God wanted a man of peace to build the temple. God promised that David's son would be the one to build that temple.

It would seem normal for anyone who received this word to be honored, but complacent. If we were not to build the temple, then we may as well take it easy for the rest of our lives. That is the opposite of what David did. Even though David could not build the temple, he still made it the obsession of his heart for the rest of his life. He would spend the wealth of his kingdom from this point forward to make preparations for it to be built after his death.

DAVID'S RESPONSE
7:18-29

When David heard the promises God had made to him, it probably made the denial of building the temple seem a small thing. David was humbled beyond imagination to have God promise and everlasting kingdom for him. How can someone even wrap their mind around that?

David not only expressed how humbled he was that God would promise such things to him, but he boldly approached God's throne of grace. He reiterated that he understood that it was for God's glory that He would promote David and his family line, and he asked boldly for God to make good on that promise. David looked to the glory of God to fill the earth and reach all the nations through this promise, something alluded to by the prophet Amos.

> "In that day
> I will restore David's fallen shelter—
> I will repair its broken walls

and restore its ruins—
and will rebuild it as it used to be,
so that they may possess the remnant of Edom
and all the nations that bear my name, "
declares the Lord, who will do these things.

Amos 9:11-12

It was the Lord's plan to use David's family line to redeem all the earth through Israel, and David had at least a modest understanding of this. How great is that salvation through a Jewish king named Jesus for us today!

2 SAMUEL CHAPTER 8

DAVID THE CONQUERER
8:1-14

David became one of the most powerful military rulers of history. Everywhere he went, he seemed to conquer with ease. He started out as king in Hebron ridding Israel of the Philistines who had recently taken the land. After moving to Jerusalem he continued to push them back and eventually went and took Gath and Ziklag from them (1 Samuel 27:6).

David continued to fight against those who were around Israel and took territory all the way to the Euphrates River in what is modern-day Iraq and Syria. Then he stopped. He eventually stopped conquering and rested, something no other great military commander would have ever considered. Alexander the great was said to have died of a broken heart because he couldn't think of anything else to conquer. Rome, the Greeks and the Persians would all set their eyes on perpetual conquering, but David stopped. Why?

Once David had taken all the land that God had promised to Moses, he stopped. David did not take any land for himself to make his name great, but instead took only the land that God had promised to Israel to make the name of the Lord great.

Our author does not tell us of any difficulty that David had in conquering, but our text does mention an unusual amount of cruelty David showed to the Moabites. When David was running from Saul, he took his parents to the king of Moab and asked for their protection, since David's family was directly descended from Ruth, a Moabite (1 Samuel 22:3). Although not referenced in scripture, non-biblical texts tell us that at some point the king of Moab, possibly motivated by a hopeful alliance with Saul, put David's parents to death. It seems that David's cruelty to the Moabites was his vengeance for killing his parents in cold blood after their king's promise of safety for them.

All of the plunder from conquering the surrounding nations David dedicated to the Lord. What we will find out later is that this meant David stored all the gold and silver and bronze near Jericho in preparation for the temple.

KINGDOM OFFICIALS
8:15-18

Chapter eight concludes with a list of the officials of David's kingdom at its outset. Like many political administrations, things would change over time. Sometimes things like a recorder and secretary may seem insignificant tasks in the kingdom of God, but what an honor that these men's names are recorded for all eternity in scripture. We should always seek to fulfill the assignments the Lord gives us with willingness and faithfulness.

The last mention is of the Kerethites and Pelethites. Nobody knows for certain who these groups were, but most scholars think that they were a group of mercenary warriors, possibly Philistines from the area around Ziklag where David spent his last few pre-king years.

Don't forget to read 2 Samuel this week!
Visit 10WeekBible.com for more resources including daily podcasts, videos and more.

41

2 Samuel 9–11

Study Questions

1. Why was it so important for David to show kindness to Jonathan's family?

2. How do you think Ziba felt about having to give everything to Mephibosheth?

3. Why would David want to show the son of Nahash the Ammonite kindness?

4. What was the result of the war with the Ammonites?

5. Do you think David should have been off fighting with Joab in the siege of Rabbah?

6. At what point do you think things became sinful in David's relationship with Bathsheba?

7. Why do you think David tried so hard to cover up his affair with Bathsheba? Why do you think he ultimately resorted to having Uriah killed?

COMMENTARY NOTES

2 SAMUEL CHAPTER 9

MEPHIBOSHETH
9:1-8

Time and wars can make us forget our old promises and commitments, and here David is somehow reminded years later of the covenant he made with Jonathan. David sent for and found a man named Ziba, who had been a servant in Saul's palace.

Ziba, no doubt, must have been terrified to be called into David's presence. Even though David had made it as clear as possible that he had no intention of going to war with Saul and his descendants, rumors and conventional wisdom probably still reigned. When David asked Ziba if he could show kindness to someone in the house of Saul, he probably had to think twice as to whether David was establishing a ruse to weed out any remaining family members or if he was really serious. We will find out later that it seems Ziba could have cared less either way.

Ziba told David of Jonathan's son Mephibosheth who was living on the east side of the Jordan river in a friend's house. David sent for Mephibosheth and had him brought to Jerusalem. When he came before David, he fell down on his face to present himself. He must have felt as if he needed to beg for his life. He was five when his father died and he was rendered lame, so he probably had no idea of the secret covenant David had made with Jonathan.

David told him not to be afraid of him. He gave back to him all the belongings of his Grandfather's household that Ziba had been continuing to serve and enjoy. He invited him to eat at his table and be in his presence. Mephibosheth's life changed in a dramatic way in just a day!

ZIBA
9:9-13

Things did not go so well for Ziba, however. Since Mephibosheth had been in exile, there was no one left in Saul's household to enjoy the inherited wealth. Ziba and his family had been living off of what Saul had left behind for some time and he had probably become accustomed to living well. In a matter of months, Ziba had gone from being a servant of Saul to practically owning everything he had acquired during his kingship. Now, David was taking everything back and giving it to Mephibosheth.

From an ownership perspective, this was the right thing to do. From the perspective of David's promise to Jonathan, this was the right thing to do. From a practical and human-nature standpoint, this may not have been the wisest moment for king David.

Since Mephibosheth would continue living in Jerusalem with David and all his inheritance was in the area around Gibeah, Ziba was now reduced to working for Mephibosheth at a distance. He was forced to continue working and administering the land just as he had been before, but now none of it was his. This kind of frustration would lead Ziba to plot a way to get his fortune back, and he would lay in wait for the opportune time.

2 SAMUEL CHAPTER 10

DAVID'S VICTORIES
10:1-19

This passage has caused scholars fits because David decided to show the son of Nahash kindness. Nahash, king of the Ammonites was the same man who had terrorized Israel in the days when Saul became king. We were told back in 1 Samuel 11 that Nahash had put out one eye of every Israelite on the east side of the Jordan river and then laid siege to Jabesh Gilead. Why on earth would David want to show this man kindness?

According to some extra-biblical texts, when David's family was murdered by the king of Moab, one of David's brothers escaped and fled to Nahash. Nahash offered David's brother refuge, and this may be the kindness David says Nahash had shown to him. We don't know for sure, but regardless of why David decided to show Hanun kindness, this is one more reason why international politics, even three thousand years ago, are a strange and risky business.

David's decision to show kindness to Hanun was not well received. They chose not to kill the messengers

David had sent, but to severely humiliate them. We see from this passage just how important it was in those days for men to wear their beards long, so don't believe any of those statues and paintings where David is clean-shaven.

Before David had time to think about how to respond, Hanun hired a tremendous mercenary army to defend Ammon. When David heard about it, he and Joab and the entire army marched to meet them at their capitol, Rabbah. War never goes exactly as planned, but here we find the only story of a dire military situation during David's kingship. From reading scripture, it seems like David never encountered any obstacles fighting other armies. That may not be the case, but here we see that things did not go as planned.

When they arrived, Joab realized that they had been tricked and were now surrounded. He put his brother Abishai in charge of half the army and they fought on two fronts. They ended up being victorious, but David must not have wanted to lay siege to the city and take it from Hanun, so they returned to Jerusalem.

The Arameans must have seen a weakness in David's army in the battle that day, and even though they lost, they must have thought they could win if given another chance. Their king, Hadadezer, brought the rest of the army to the West and prepared to attack Israel. David heard about this and mobilized Israel to meet them before they crossed into the land.

Now our author takes us back to how we are used to reading about David's victories: complete and without

47

incidence. We can be sure that every battle David and his armies fought was difficult, but this was such a resounding victory there is no mention of the dead of Israel. Imagine what forty thousand dead foot soldiers strewn about a vast countryside must have looked like. Imagine what it must have smelled like.

The Arameans apparently had a large number of smaller nations around them that had been paying them tribute for peace, and now they realized it was David they needed to be paying. Not only did the Arameans lose thousands of soldiers and their commander, but they also lost a tremendous amount of control and financial support.

All that control and financial support continued to grow during David's lifetime and would establish a kingdom and kingship of almost mythical wealth, one that is still spoken of today in superlative manner. Solomon was to become the greatest and wealthiest king in history because of what his father David had done during his lifetime.

2 SAMUEL CHAPTER 11

BATHSHEBA
11:1-5

The next spring, David decided to send Joab back out and finish the job with the Ammonites. The army loaded up and headed to Rabbah to begin a prolonged siege of the city while David stayed behind in Jerusalem. Our author does not always tell us what battles David himself travelled to, but we do know that at some point his men begged him to stop fighting with them for the sake of Israel.

2 Samuel 21 tells of an encounter with the Philistines, possibly during the reign of David in Hebron, where one of Goliath's brothers almost killed David and from that point on the army wouldn't allow David to fight with them anymore.

So the idea that David was supposed to be off at war when his tryst with Bathsheba happened may not actually be the case. Our author is speaking more to the timing of when this happened more so than David not being where he was supposed to be. We should always strive to be where we are supposed to be, but practically applying that notion is a lot harder than it sounds on paper. We cannot always know when we should have been at that dinner party instead of staying home, or vice-versa.

Our consciences (the Holy Spirit) tell us when we are in a place we definitely should not be, but it is so much more challenging to know the difference between two perfectly valid places to be at the same time. David's problem wasn't that he stayed home, but that when his conscience screamed out to stop looking at Bathsheba, he persisted. That was the very moment he crossed into that place where he wasn't supposed to be. There is also something to be said for staying busy as opposed to having empty time on our hands to view and then obsess over a naked woman (or substitute whatever you want here) in our neighbor's yard.

We cannot always help what our eyes see against our will. It doesn't seem that David was trying to be a peeping tom that day, but he decided he wanted what he had seen and became fixated on sleeping with her. David already had a harem, so his next question still could have been innocent enough. Maybe she was available, he thought, so he inquired about her. When the messenger told David who she was, that is when he should have been stopped in his tracks. The fact that David still persisted after he knew who she was speaks to the sinful intentions in David's heart and how deep his lust had grown.

She was the wife of Uriah the Hittite, one of David's mighty men. 2 Samuel 23 tells us that Uriah was one of the mightiest thirty warriors in David's army and someone who had probably been with him from the days when he was hiding from Saul in the cave. Uriah was a foreigner, but he had been fiercely loyal to David for at least a decade. The fact that David was willing to have an affair with her is a sad moment for David.

But Bathsheba wasn't just the wife of Uriah, she was the daughter of Eliam, the granddaughter of a man named Ahithophel, David's chief counsel. David was messing around with all kinds of powerful forces, and it was going to come back to bite him many times over. Instead of honoring his loyal warrior and chief counsel and letting the matter rest, he had her brought to him and he impregnated her.

Some want to believe that Bathsheba was basically raped by David. Others say that Bathsheba was a willing participant. Our author remains silent on behalf of

Bathsheba, so we should never make too much of what the Bible remains silent on. What is important, and the prophet Nathan will point this out, is that David was the most powerful man on earth at the time. That kind of power comes with incredible responsibility, and David completely neglected that. If we are to evaluate the weight of sin, even if Bathsheba was willing, the weight of David's sin was so much greater than hers it is hardly worth comparing.

And that sin was going to continue piling up.

THE COVER-UP
11:6-13

When Bathsheba told David she was pregnant, he sprang to action. He called Uriah home from the siege of Rabbah so that he would make love to Bathsheba and everyone would think that the child was his. Never mind that the math would not have added up very well for her pregnancy—David wasn't thinking that far ahead yet.

David personally greeted Uriah and sent him home and had a gift delivered to his house. The next day, David must have been shocked when he found out that Uriah hadn't gone home. Even more shocking was the fact that Uriah refused to do the very thing David had intended for him to do and said it out loud in his presence!

David knew that Uriah's will was too strong and that he was a man of devout principle, so he knew he wasn't going to sleep with Bathsheba unless he intervened in another way. That evening, David invited Uriah to the palace to party with him and made sure that Uriah got punch drunk.

Unfortunately for David, Uriah was still too in control of his faculties and refused to go home and experience the pleasures that his fellow soldiers were currently going without on the battle field.

What happened next is simply tragic. David penned a letter to Joab to have Uriah intentionally killed in battle. Then he gave Uriah the letter! How David must have ached on the inside knowing that he had sent his loyal mighty man on his way with his own death warrant in hand, unbeknownst to him! David would later write in a Psalm that his bones ached while he wrestled with this secret sin.

Blessed is the one
whose transgressions are forgiven,
whose sins are covered.
Blessed is the one
whose sin the Lord does not count against them
and in whose spirit is no deceit.
When I kept silent,
my bones wasted away
through my groaning all day long.
For day and night
your hand was heavy on me;
my strength was sapped
as in the heat of summer.

Then I acknowledged my sin to you
and did not cover up my iniquity.
I said, "I will confess
my transgressions to the Lord."
And you forgave
the guilt of my sin.

Psalm 32:1-5

David's plan fore Uriah worked, though. Joab put Uriah next to the wall of Rabbah and Uriah died, as well as the other men who were around Uriah. It wasn't just Uriah that died, but several unsuspecting innocent souls that got caught up in David's web of lies.

If the sin of adultery and murder weren't enough, David was now bound to Joab, his wicked and ruthless nephew he would rather have not had in charge of the army. Joab had his "get out of jail free card" from David now, and it would be a plague to David for years to come.

Joab sent a messenger boy to David to tell him of the casualties in their secret code and warned the young man that David may get angry when he heard the news. But when the messenger told David of the casualties and Uriah, the king didn't even feign his anger. Instead, he made possibly the most callous and horrible statement of his life.

"The sword devours." That would be a phrase he would regret for many years to come.

Like Abigail, David "graciously" married Bathsheba

after the ritual time of mourning was over for her late husband. Within the confines of his palace, David was probably able to easily conceal the fact that Bathsheba delivered a healthy baby boy at six to seven months instead of nine. No one was the wiser, and David had gotten away with it all.

Except that the One who had given David all this favor and victory in the first place was the only one who it all mattered to, and He was not happy at all.

Don't forget to read 2 Samuel this week!
Visit 10WeekBible.com for more resources including daily podcasts, videos and more.

2 SAMUEL 12–13

STUDY QUESTIONS

1. Why do you think the Lord had Nathan tell David a story instead of just saying He knew what David had done outright?

2. What made David's outcome here different than that of Saul and Eli before him?

3. Why do you think David fasted for the baby even after the Lord's prophetic word to him? Why do you think the baby died?

4. Why didn't David want Rabbah renamed to Joabville?

5. Why did Amnon hate Tamar after he slept with her? Why do you think David's nephew helped Amnon do such a terrible thing?

6. If David was furious about Tamar's rape, why didn't he do anything about it? What would you have done if you were in David's shoes?

7. Why did Absalom wait two years to kill Amnon? Who did he flee to?

Commentary Notes

2 Samuel Chapter 12

The Lord Knows
12:1-14

Jesus said that the reason He spoke in parables was so that people would not understand what He was trying to say. This wasn't because He didn't want people to know Him, but because He only wanted the hearts hungry enough to ask Him directly what He meant to know Him. He wanted the humble hearts to draw near to Him and the proud hearts to grow further away so that they would be challenged by the pain in their life and then humbly come to Him.

> *This is why I speak to them in parables: "Though seeing, they do not see; though hearing, they do not hear or understand.*
>
> *Matthew 13:13*

Nathan came to David this day in the same spirit. Keep in mind that when Nathan came to David, months had passed. David believed he had gotten away with all this, and even his conscience was probably beginning to wane about the affair and murder. We read these two stories back-to-back, but for David, nothing could be further from the front of his mind when Nathan begins this story of injustice.

As a shepherd, David could picture exactly what

Nathan was saying to him. David probably grew to like one or two of the sheep he kept for his father in his youth. His father was wealthy and had lots of sheep, but this man who only had one probably resonated with David. That is why David's anger flared up when Nathan told him of the man who had mercilessly taken this poor little lamb.

David understood that Nathan was speaking to him as a judge of Israel, so David's pronouncement of death was extreme overkill in this case, but it speaks to just how well Nathan's story connected with him and how little David was able to perceive about his own situation. It was also a prophetic pronouncement by David of the fate that he himself deserved.

Nathan had known David for years and the two were probably close. Nathan and Gad were two prophets who spent many years with David and most scholars think they were the ones responsible for writing and compiling much of the book of Samuel. Even still, this must have been a nerve-racking moment for Nathan. If David had been willing to kill Uriah, one of his most faithful warriors, would he have been willing to kill him too?

Nathan obeyed the Lord even still and confronted David with the intensity the Lord felt over this issue. He told David what the Lord said as straight as anyone possibly could.

What the Lord spoke to David sounds nearly as harsh as what He spoke to Eli back in 1 Samuel 2. God promised that David's family would be ravaged by war, strife and death. Imagine being in David's shoes at that very moment hearing the terrible news that the Lord Himself was speaking to you! What is very different between David and Eli, however, are their responses.

Eli seemed to just take what the Lord told him and moved on with life as if fate was directing him. David, on the other hand, immediately repented. David's heart of repentance is amazing, but it is not going to spare him from the full consequences of his sin. The Lord did spare his life, though.

It is worth pointing out here that many people use this to view God as someone that enjoys "shaking us over hell on a rotten stick," but this is not the case. The difference between most of us and David is that David was king of Israel. God had supernaturally protected him and then given him the Kingdom of His holy people. He was a world leader put in place through supernatural providence. There is a greater accountability among leaders with the Lord.

> *From everyone who has been given much, much will be demanded; and from the one who has been entrusted with much, much more will be asked.*
>
> *Luke 12:48*

This does not give us who may not be world leaders a license to sin, but instead puts into perspective the severity of the punishment David was forced to endure. It is not a good idea to test the limits of God's patience with us, but we can be free of the lie that God is just itching to smite us at the first slip-up. David's was no small mistake, and he bore this great responsibility that Jesus spoke of in Luke. We should all take the callings and responsibilities the Lord has given us seriously, but we should not think that God will treat everyone just as He did David for small missteps along the way (again, David's was not small).

THE BABY
12:15-25

One of the most difficult aspects of this story to deal with is the fact that the Lord took the baby's life. On one hand, the Lord has promise that no one would die for the sins of their fathers, but only for their own sins. On the other hand, the Lord has said that the sins of fathers will be visited on subsequent generations.

> *Parents are not to be put to death for their children, nor children put to death for their parents; each will die for their own sin.*

> *Deuteronomy 24:16*

> *You shall not bow down to them or worship them; for I, the Lord your God, am a jealous God, punishing the children for the sin of the parents to the third and fourth generation of those who hate me, but showing love to a thousand generations of those who love me and keep my commandments.*

> *Deuteronomy 5:9-10*

On the surface, this looks very confusing. God spoke it both ways in the book of Deuteronomy, so which is it? The simple answer is that it is both. God will allow children to suffer for the sins of their parents and ancestors, but at the same time there is freedom from such suffering for those who break that chain of sin.

On a practical level, we see this all the time. Far too many children today live in a hellish existence because of their parents' sins and lifestyles, yet for those who reject their parents' ways and turn to the Lord, God gives freedom and grace.

But none of that explains why God chose to kill the baby who had no chance to choose right or wrong. When we find things like this in scripture, it puts us in a place of tension we often try to escape prematurely. Many people want to explain this away so they don't have to deal with the fears they have that God really isn't good. Some even come away with the conclusion that God must not be good if He would do such a thing.

Instead of letting a story like this offend us, we should seek the Lord, just as David did in the midst of a pronouncement of death, and be very slow to develop a theology based off of something we do not understand. God could have easily explained why the son must die, but He chose not to, only stating that it would happen. David took that opportunity to repent and fast and seek the Lord to spare the baby's life.

David was the one to receive such a devastating prophecy from God, but he didn't think God was wicked for such a thing. In fact, David knew that God was so good He may change His mind if David cried out, so for the entire time the baby was sick, David sought a God he knew to be very forgiving and gracious. The more important takeaway from this story than the baby dying is David's confidence in God's goodness even amidst circumstances he couldn't understand or control.

When the baby died, David resolved to quickly accept the outcome and immediately went to worship the Lord. At no point did David accuse the Lord of wrongdoing, but he trusted His goodness and justness.

And don't worry if this is surprising or difficult to understand. David's attendants were just as surprised. That is because when we grow closer to God like David, we see His goodness in the midst of some of the most terrible places. Even in the midst of his terrible sin, David still knew how good God was. Most people struggle to accept God's goodness in all situations, and David is a shining example of how a very flawed human can experience the depth and knowledge of God's goodness, something we too can have today if we choose to seek Him.

Bathsheba became pregnant again and gave birth to Solomon, but God was not content with that name. He sent Nathan the prophet to David again and told him that God had changed his name to Jedidiah, which means "loved by the Lord." God wanted David and Bathsheba to know that the fate of the first child was not going to be a continual curse over their lives.

The fact that God loved Solomon is not a pronouncement that He didn't love other children or people, but a gesture of the greatest kindness to David and Bathsheba so that they would never doubt God's love for them or their children.

DEFEATING RABBAH
12:26-31

It may be easy to forget where this all started, but all this time Joab and the army had been continuing to lay siege to Rabbah, the capitol of Ammon. Once Joab had secured its fall, he notified the very absent David that if he didn't show up to finish the job Joab was going to rename the city after himself. David could tell the irritation in Joab's tone in the message and it probably terrified David to think of any town on earth being named after Joab.

David quickly mustered the army and joined the siege until the city fell. By this time, it seems that the siege must have gone on for over a year at least. The people were probably too weak to put up much of a fight and the city fell without incident.

The most remarkable bit of plunder David acquired from Rabbah was a crown of ridiculous weight. He took the seventy-five pound crown of the king and placed it on his head, which sounds a lot like a dare given to him by his troops. It was probably an incredibly expensive show-piece not really intended to be worn, but in the excitement and joyfulness of taking the city, David put it on for show to prove that it wouldn't snap his neck.

Then David sent his men to alert the people of Ammon that they were going to be allowed to live, but that they were henceforth his laborers for public works projects. Given David's treatment of the neighboring Moabites, they were more than likely willing to accept this arrangement.

2 SAMUEL CHAPTER 13

THE PROPHECY BEGINS TO COME TRUE
13:1-22

Nathan had prophesied to David about strife, war and death in his family, and now we are told the beginning of that trouble that would befall David's family. Amnon became infatuated with his half-sister Tamar, but was powerless to do anything about it. Amnon was not much different than David in his instant lust for Bathsheba, but Amnon was not a king who could do whatever he wanted. He knew his father David would not allow him to marry his sister, so it made him sick.

Just to be clear, the kind of love Amnon felt was not true love, but pure physical lust. The Bible calls it love here only because that is how Amnon would have described it, not because that is what it truly was.

It isn't clear what Jonadab's motivations were for his advice to Amnon, but he clearly had a mind bent on wickedness. He convinced Amnon to rape Tamar, possibly one of the top five worst things to happen in the books of Samuel. Unfortunately Amnon's lust had been sinfully kindled to the point that this was perfectly acceptable to him now.

Amnon's plan was a thinly veiled ruse to get what he wanted. Poor, naive Tamar must not have seen it coming, but it seems that everyone knew of Amnon's desire for her because of what Absalom would later say to her. After Amnon had gotten her alone, he physically overpowered her. As she knew what was inevitably coming, she tried to reason with him. In desperation, she tried to buy time by convincing Amnon that David would let them be married if he wanted, something he certainly doubted since he hadn't even asked up to this point.

As soon as Amnon had finished having his way with Tamar, he became very angry. The knowledge of what he had done and her unwillingness to satisfy him made him hate her now. It literally took seconds for Amnon to go from thinking he loved Tamar to hating her intensely. Again Tamar tried to reason with him not to send her away, but his callous, sinful heart wouldn't listen.

When Absalom found her, he knew what had happened. He advised Tamar to keep it quiet and then he let her live in his house the rest of his life so he could provide for her. He didn't ask her to keep it quiet because he wanted to preserve the family relations, but so he could exact his revenge on Amnon at a time that pleased him most. Absalom was on one hand a protective and loving big brother, and on the other hand a revengeful rage-monster lying in wait for the opportune time to kill his brother.

Just like Nathan had prophesied, none of this was done in secret. David found out about what Amnon had done and he was furious, but he did nothing. Years had passed since Nathan's prophecy, so David may not have put the two together, but this was the act that was eventually going to lead to his greatest trouble. As a loving father, he was powerless to punish his eldest son for such an action.

AMNON'S MURDER
13:23-38

Absalom let two years go by before he hatched a plan to kill Amnon. Absalom had no desire to kill Amnon in secret; he wanted everyone to know who did it and why. He was so sure he wanted to kill Amnon in public that he even invited his father David to the event he was planning on throwing specifically to kill Amnon at. It may have been that Absalom planned to kill his father at the same event because he was so angry that David had never done anything about Tamar.

David didn't want to go for some reason and his excuse was that his entourage would cost Absalom too much money to feed if they all came. Amnon, as David's eldest son and first in line to ascend to the throne, was in the inner circle of David's leadership. Absalom knew that Amnon wouldn't come to his party only on his invitation, so he asked David to send Amnon in his place to attend the phony celebration.

David was initially suspicious of why Absalom would be so intent on having Amnon there, but he eventually decided to send him as the king's emissary to the party. Absalom made sure that Amnon got good and drunk during the event so he would be unable to fight back or flee when he knew what was about to happen. Then, with little fanfare, Absalom's servants carried out the plan they had been given before the meal started.

Before David's others sons could get back to Jerusalem, word of what happened had preceded them. David was told that Absalom had killed everyone, and he was overcome. The rush of emotions must have been too much for David to deal with, so he collapsed on the floor. It was at that point that his nephew, Jonadab, spoke up.

Jonadab was certainly playing things both ways. He was the one who had convinced Amnon to rape Tamar in the first place, and now here he was trying to be the bearer of good news for David by convincing him that only Amnon was dead. He was certainly the closest to the events that had happened, but why on earth was he in David's court? How had he weasled his way into such a high position?

Jonadab was right, but it was still little consolation to David. The heir apparent to his throne was now dead, and his family was in upheaval.

Absalom fled to his father-in-law, the king of David's first political alliance, Geshur. King Talmai was Absalom's grandfather and he stayed with him for three years.

After David had gotten over Amnon's death, he missed Absalom, the next-eldest son and new heir to the throne. This would begin a very tenuous relationship between David and Absalom. David loved his son dearly, but he was too angry at him for Amnon's murder to send for him. It would be many more years before they would see each other again, and then only for a brief moment.

6

2 SAMUEL 14-15

STUDY QUESTIONS

1. After all he had done, why do you think David wanted Absalom back?

2. Why did Joab plan an elaborate ruse to get Absalom back instead of just directly addressing David about the situation?

3. After he came back, why didn't David want to see Absalom?

4. Why did Absalom set fire to Joab's field? Have you ever done anything similar (but maybe not quite as extreme) to get someone's attention?

5. Why do you think Absalom spent so much money on having a chariot and an entourage to travel with him?

6. Why do you think David didn't see what was coming? Why did he turn a blind eye to Absalom's activities before open rebellion and civil war?

7. Why do you think David thought he had to flee Jerusalem immediately?

8. Why did David send Hushai back to be Abaslom's advisor?

Commentary Notes

2 Samuel Chapter 14

The Ruse
14:1-22

When Joab was not out with the army on assignment, which happened less these days since David had secured all the land the Lord had promised Moses, he sat in David's court and ate at his table. Day after day Joab listened as David bemoaned what had happened to his family and how much he missed Absalom. Joab knew that David didn't like him and he wanted to change that. He wanted to lift David's spirits, but knew that if he requested directly to go and get Absalom, David would refuse.

So Joab hatched a plan. He took a play out of God and Nathan's playbook and decided to use it against David. Joab hired a woman from far away that he was sure David wouldn't suspect and sent her to him to gain a judgment from the nation's top judge, the king himself. Joab, however, wasn't nearly as creative as God, and the story he fed this woman was much less original than the one Nathan had delivered to David years before.

As she told David of the situation that had transpired between her two fictional sons, he extended grace to her and pardoned the murderous son so she would not be left childless. David probably did not suspect anything at this point, but again, Joab was not going to be subtle.

After David assured her that he himself would intervene on her behalf if anyone persisted in asking for her murderer son being brought to justice, she persisted with another request.

The woman then lashed out at David for being "the man" in her story. She proceeded to speak the words that Joab had put in her mouth about bringing Abasolom back, and David immediately knew what was going on. The entire time this woman was in front of David, Joab was in the room listening, possibly finding it hard not to wince when she got his script a little wrong.

When David asked her to tell him if it was in fact Joab behind all this, she came clean. Probably without ever turning his head to look at Joab, he spoke to Joab while maintaining eye contact with the Tekoan woman. He told Joab to go to Geshur and get Absalom and bring him back to Jerusalem.

When Joab heard this, he fell on the ground in between David and this woman. He wasn't so much as grateful that David was willing to bring Absalom back as he was that David had actually listened to a bit of advice he was giving to him. Joab knew all too well that David didn't want him in charge of the army and would have ditched Joab at the first opportune moment. For Joab, this moment was all about trying to gain a little more favor with his uncle and maintain his position as commander.

Absalom Returns
14:23-24

Joab went to Talmai to fetch Absalom. David most likely sent an entourage to his father-in-law to bring Absalom back. Expecting a greeting from his father upon returning, Absalom went with Joab and the entourage. He was going to be deeply disappointed.

Here we see just how conflicted David was with his family now. He had desperately longed to see Absalom again, but when Joab was on the way back with him David sent word that Joab was to take him to his house and not to the palace. Now that David was faced with the reality of seeing Absalom, he didn't want to.

Imagine the tension David felt to see his eldest living son, but also to bring justice he felt was demanded of him as the nation's top judge. David knew that he had effectively pardoned his own son while he had pronounced death on countless others during the course of his kingship and judgeship. That inner conflict showed out when David told Joab that he wasn't ready to see Absalom's face.

Absalom's Pain
14:25-27

Absalom settled into Jerusalem and immediately started making friends. It sounds like women would have flocked to see him shirtless at the beach from our author's description of him. As he reestablished himself at home in Jerusalem, people took note of him and liked having him around. He was the best-looking man in town, and he was certainly willing to honor the attention everyone was giving him, as we will soon find out.

Absalom would grow out his hair extremely long and make a big deal about it when he would have it cut. He would have someone weigh it to prove that he was such a physical specimen that he could grow five pounds of hair in a year. Again, Absalom was all too willing to make a show of himself in front of the people to increase his personal fame.

In a break of cultural protocol, our author gives us a bit of information about Absalom's family. Seldom were girl children listed by name when a genealogy was given in scripture, and we have here with Absalom one of the only times where sons go unnamed and only the daughter's name is told to us.

Absalom's pain and anger over his sister Tamar ran deeply. In naming his daughter Tamar, he sought to atone for the evil that had been done to his sister by giving her a name who would never have children. Absalom may have been a terribly troubled young man, but no one could accuse him of being a bad older brother.

THE MEETING
14:28-33

Absalom carried on for two years like this before he became tired of living in the shadows. He asked Joab for a meeting, the one who had made a big deal about bringing him home from Geshur in the first place, but Joab ignored him. It was hard for Joab to make a good excuse for this, since they were next-door neighbors! Absalom sent for Joab twice before taking matters into his own hands.

When at first you don't succeed, burn something down! (but don't, really) Absalom wasn't interested in being subtle. In those days even those who were given a salary and provided for at the king's table still grew their own food. Joab had his own fields to provide for his family, and Absalom set fire to this. It probably would have sufficed to burn Joab's mailbox down, but Absalom wasn't going to let Joab have any excuses to ignore him anymore.

Setting his field on fire got Joab's attention quickly. In a 3,000 year-old version of "What the heck, man?," Joab showed up at Absalom's house to have a word with him. Knowing that if he didn't do what he asked, Absalom may burn down everything he owned, Joab agreed to go to king David on his behalf.

This all led to a very brief but tender meeting be-tween David and Absalom. David kissing his son was more than just a fatherly act of love; it made official the pardon David had already unofficially extended to him. Absalom was now fully restored to his position as a son of David in the nation's eyes, something Absa-lom was going to milk for everything it was worth in the coming years.

2 SAMUEL CHAPTER 15

ABSALOM'S RISE
15:1-6

After his full pardon from David, Absalom began to enact a plan he had probably already created. He established his new position as a restored son of David by buying himself a large entourage. If you ever want to create the illusion of being important, just hire a bunch of people to surround you as servants. It may cost you everything you own, but people will most certainly look at you with respect. Depending on your financial situation, that respect may not last very long. In Absalom's case, as the eldest son of the king, he had an almost unlimited supply of money.

What Absalom did with his entourage, though, is quite interesting. Instead of using them to attend parties and show off how important and beautiful he was, he used them to make his ad-hoc court look more official. Every day Absalom got them all up early and went with them in his chariot to the most prominent gate of Jerusalem to meet and greet the people.

Absalom would turn on the charm for everyone who was coming to Jerusalem to seek David as an arbiter over their situation. He would lament the fact that he wasn't judge over the land, which he most certainly should be, and then go on to give them a judgment anyway. Like a politician who makes lots of promises with little intention on following through, Absalom made lots of promises that endeared him to the people.

He would make sure that he always answered the people who showed up for judgment favorably, even when the other party didn't show up. With Absalom, every road would get fixed, every hand shaken and every baby kissed. In fact, Absalom would not allow anyone to bow before him, as was customary before the king. He wanted everyone to think of him as the peoples' leader.

It would take nearly three thousand years for politicians to figure out what Absalom knew then. He became a populist leader and stole the hearts of the people with no real intention to help them. This was all about Absalom. In all those years of exile, he had convinced himself that he would make such a better king than his father who failed to act on behalf of his little sister.

THE REBELLION
15:7-12

After four years of Absalom's plan to steal the hearts of the people, he decided it was time to take the plan to the next level. In all that time, David had never said anything to him, even though his advisors must have raised some questions. Maybe David thought that Absalom was trying to work himself into his role as king after David was gone. Maybe David just didn't have it in him to stop what he knew Absalom was doing. Whatever his reasons for allowing Absalom to carry on as he did, David didn't see what was coming next when he asked to take a large entourage to Hebron.

Absalom knew that it would sound like he was going to celebrate and pay a vow back in the place of his birth. His real intention was to establish himself as the new king in the place where David had reigned for seven years. Hebron was a royal city, and he wanted his throne established there until he could take Jerusalem for himself.

Because he had gotten the blessing of his father, Absalom invited two hundred nobles from Israel to go with him for his celebration. They didn't know what Absalom had planned, but he knew that with their presence it would look like they were lending their support behind what was happening. He also knew that with the show of force he would have on hand that they wouldn't dare oppose him openly during the ceremony. He was leveraging their clout in Israel to establish himself in the eyes of the people from the other tribes of Israel who were there.

Absalom proclaimed himself ask king there in Hebron, something that David surely heard about. Initially, it seems that David did nothing, but when Ahithophel went to join Absalom, things were out of control. His counselors that were still with him warned him that Absalom's rebellion was now more than a petulant son self-identifying as king. This was real and the people of Israel were convinced that Absalom had taken over the kingdom.

A TIME TO RUN
15:13-22

When Ahithophel defected to Absalom, David knew he couldn't initially stop what was going on. He knew that Ahithophel had chosen the side that he thought would win if there were open conflict for Jerusalem, and David knew that Ahithophel was one of the wisest counselors he had. He wasn't wrong.

Remember that Ahithophel was Bathsheba's grandfather. At this point it doesn't seem like God had proclaimed that Solomon would become king, or at least if He had, David hadn't told anyone else yet. Ahithophel had probably harbored resentment against David all these years, and now that there was an opportunity to overthrow him, he was happy to be a part of it.

Ahithophel knew how David thought. He knew David's strategies and his tactics. David knew that if they didn't flee Jerusalem that very instant, that Ahithophel would have advised Absalom to have the people of Israel surround Jerusalem and cut off any ability for him to escape. With Jerusalem under siege and cut off, David would have had no way to communicate with the people of Israel and Absalom would be left to rewrite David's history in their eyes as he saw fit.

The only way to survive was to flee immediately. It can be hard to understand from this passage the urgency that all this was taking place with because our author pauses to tell us about some of the conversations David had with certain people. It may seem like David was casually talking with them from his throne while his attendants packed his bags, but that is not what was going on. The conversations in this chapter are literally happening as David is running away from Jerusalem with the people running alongside him. This was as intense a moment as any Hollywood movie would make it out to be.

Most scholars think that the Kerethites and Pelethites were mercenaries from Philistia that David had befriended during his time there. There is some evidence that they may have even been his own palace guard, a means of protecting himself from anyone with Hebrew blood from trying to overthrow him from within. Just the day before another Philistine had defected to him with a large militia, and Ittai refused to leave David's side.

In the midst of David's lowest moment we find out something remarkable about him. In his youth, he had been sung about as having killed tens of thousands of Philistines. He had killed their champion, Goliath, and later in Samuel we will be told that he and his men killed Goliath's four brothers of nearly equal stature. David was no friend to the Philistines, but still somehow more and more of them loved David. Why?

When the righteous thrive, the people rejoice; when the wicked rule, the people groan.

Proverbs 29:2

We often think of these other nations as a monolithic bloc of evil people, but that isn't what they were. Just like anywhere else, there were wicked people and good people. Leaders like Goliath, Achish and the other nobles of Philistia were wicked. That meant that the good people had to hide out as long as they were in power. When David overthrew the Philistine's control over Israel, he did take away their sovereignty, but he also removed all the wicked leaders and replaced them with a vassal government under his control.

It may have taken a few years, but things in Philistia got better for everyone. Hundreds of them came and joined David's palace guard and found him to be a great man. Ittai came the day before, and faced with the opportunity to go home and rally the Philisitnes to take advantage of David's weakness, he instead chose loyalty to the best leader the Philistines had ever known: a Hebrew.

Even with all of David's flaws, he was still a leader who followed the Lord with all his heart. Sworn enemies will prosper under the leadership of the godly. That is why David wrote this:

> *You prepare a table before me*
> *in the presence of my enemies.*
> *You anoint my head with oil;*
> *my cup overflows.*
> *Surely your goodness and love will follow me*
> *all the days of my life,*
> *and I will dwell in the house of the Lord*
> *forever.*
>
> *Psalm 23:5-6*

THE ARK STAYS
15:23-31

Zadok had the Levites load up the ark on its poles and they carried it out with David to go where he went. When David saw it and met up with Zadok, he sent them back to Jerusalem. David knew that Jerusalem was the city that God, not he, had chosen as a resting place for the ark.

David was not going to take the ark as a talisman of good luck with him; it no longer belonged to him. It belonged in Jerusalem, and David understood a little bit of God's eternal plan at this point. He knew that Israel's history had shifted to become Jerusalem-centric, and that even if wicked, blood-thirsty men were to overrun it, it was still God's chosen city and that was more important than even David's character, integrity and leadership.

David sent Zadok and Abiathar back and asked them to send their sons with word of what happened to Jerusalem. He knew that Absalom would not kill the priests or harm the ark, so he had confidence in their return.

As David left Jerusalem, all the people in the surrounding area wept, because they had a better front-row seat to see how David had led the people. They knew just what they were losing as David fled.

DAVID'S LOYAL SPIES
15:32-37

Our author here references that at the top of the

Mount of Olives, people used to worship the Lord. This is referring to people worshipping God on high places, something He strictly prohibited. David put an end to this practice and only allowed people to sacrifice at the tabernacle which was not in Jerusalem during David's reign. In the book of Kings, the author points that out during the reign of every king who allowed the practice to continue.

As David hurriedly left the city, Hushai, another of his advisors, came to him. Instead of having him come with him, David asked him to go back to Absalom and pretend to be loyal to him. David thought that if Absalom would listen to Hushai's advice, maybe he wouldn't listen to Ahithophel. We see here that David was only truly afraid of Ahithophel when it came to Absalom's rebellion.

Don't forget to read 2 Samuel this week!
Visit 10WeekBible.com for more resources including daily podcasts, videos and more.

7

2 SAMUEL 16-17

STUDY QUESTIONS

1. Have you ever had a time in your life where you felt like every wrong decision and bad thing you'd ever done came back to bite you all at once? Why do you think the Lord let David go through that? Why would He let you go through that?

2. Why did David say that the Lord told Shimei to curse him and throw rocks at him? Would you have wanted to kill him that day?

3. Why would Ahithophel advise Absalom to sleep with David's concubines he left behind?

4. Why did Ahithophel want to strike David quickly?

5. Why do you think Absalom chose to listen to Hushai's advice?

6. Why do you think Ahithophel killed himself just because Absalom took Hushai's advice instead of his?

Commentary Notes

2 Samuel Chapter 16

Never Waste a Crisis
16:1-4

Remember Ziba? Saul's servant who had inherited everything his master owned right up until King David gave it all away to Mephibosheth? That Ziba. Well, it's his turn now.

Ziba had been laying in wait for some time to get everything back that had once been his. He had been waiting for just the right time to act, running a thousand scenarios in his head of how he could do it. This crisis of David leaving Jerusalem was the perfect opportunity. Ziba surely hoped that David would never return to Jerusalem to discover the truth behind what he had done. His act of kindness was anything but genuine.

Because David was in duress and Mephibosheth wasn't there to answer for himself, David didn't think through what Ziba was telling him and gave everything of Saul's back to Ziba. It didn't make sense for Mephibosheth to think that the Israelites would restore a kingdom to him when it was Absalom who was about to rule from Jerusalem. If anything, Jerusalem was the worst place on earth for Mephibosheth to be. What better way for Absalom to establish himself by deposing his father and eliminating any others who would lay claim to the throne?

SHIMEI
16:5-14

Shimei felt emboldened in his anger and jealousy by the turn of events recently, and couldn't help himself. He showed up to watch David and his men flee Jerusalem and decided to heap curses, rocks and dirt down on them. They were walking along a path in a ravine while Shimei was above them. Shimei wasn't going to kill any of them, but he was intolerably irritating on the worst day of their lives.

Shimei wasn't just some crazy drunk, though. He was from Saul's family line. When the kingdom shifted from Saul to David, he lost everything. Saul was intensely loyal to his family, as almost all monarchs are. Shimei's family probably greatly benefited from Saul being in charge. We are never told this, but we can assume that Shimei probably held some position in Saul's government that instantly evaporated when he died.

Shimei was actually a relatively wealthy man with clout in his clan. This was more than just the insults of an angry man, it was an attempt to announce his plans to undermine David's kingdom from here on.

David and his men probably didn't know all of this at the time. To them, Shimei seemed like an angry idiot, and for a group of proud warriors, Shimei needed to be silenced. Abishai, Joab's brother, told David he was going to behead Shimei for his cursing.

In this incredibly low point for David, he showed an amazing amount of character and faith in God. David knew that everything that was happening was the discipline of the Lord for his affair and murder. He chose to trust that the Lord still loved him. He chose to let the Lord speak up for him against Shimei one day, but for now he would remain silent.

The Prophecy Fulfilled
16:15-23

Absalom entered Jerusalem with the greatest of fanfare. By this point, the people of Israel believed that he had rightfully ascended to the throne. There were only a handful of people who knew what was really going on, and they were too afraid to say much at this point.

As he entered Jerusalem, Hushai showed up. Absalom was at first hesitant to see him. He knew what good friends he and his father were. Hushai reassured Absalom by repeating the line that was circling Israel now: that God had chosen Absalom to take over. Hushai pledged his false allegiance to Absalom and he accepted it.

Almost immediately after securing the holy city Jerusalem without a fight, thanks to his father David, Absalom set out to strategize how to finish him off. He turned to Ahithophel to find out what he proposed he should do next.

Our author tells us that Ahithophel was David's most trusted advisor and that his advice was nearly equal to that of a prophet. He was a wise thinker, and very familiar with the human condition. He knew how to manipulate the public and move agendas forward. He was a master spin doctor and political analyst, the likes of which the greatest politicians of today could only wish to have in their corner.

Ahithophel's great advice was to do what all other leaders tried to do in these times of upheaval: burn their bridges. As we have seen in our study of the book of Samuel, it was somewhat common in that day that if you wanted to assume rulership via a coup, often the first act was to sleep with the outgoing ruler's wives. David had left all the concubines—those he hadn't married or had married from less than noble birth—behind in Jerusalem to care for the palace and the harem buildings in case he returned.

Ahithophel encouraged Absalom to sleep with all of them so that all Israel would no there was no going back to the way things were. There would be no reconciliation between David and Absalom. But not only did Ahithophel encourage Absalom to do this, he told him to do it out in the open! What a crude and despicable act as a coronation!

The Lord was using Ahithophel, however. Unknowingly, Ahithophel was helping Absalom fulfill exactly what Nathan the prophet had told David the Lord was going to do as punishment for the murder of Uriah.

"This is what the Lord says: 'Out of your own household I am going to bring calamity on you. Before your very eyes I will take your wives and give them to one who is close to you, and he will sleep with your wives in broad daylight. You did

it in secret, but I will do this thing in broad day-
light before all Israel.'"

2 Samuel 12:11-12

At the time, this must have seemed to be an oddly specific and grotesque word from the Lord. Now, looking back, it was even more surprisingly accurate and specific. It didn't come to pass figuratively, but entirely literally. The Lord took what David did in secret and put it on demonstration out in the open for the entire nation to see and whisper about.

2 SAMUEL CHAPTER 17

HUSHAI'S ADVICE SAVES DAVID
17:1-14

Ahithophel knew David well. He knew his personality, his weaknesses and his strategies. He knew that on this day, David would be overcome with emotion and weak from the journey. If David was allowed to rest and get his head on straight, Absalom would have little chance of defeating him.

Ahithophel knew that Absalom's only chance was to strike now. Twelve thousand men was no small number, but he knew Absalom could muster them quickly and make a short end of David. Ahithophel also recommended that they not go after anyone but David. He knew that no one in Israel wanted another protracted civil war like they had between David and Ish-Bosheth. He told Absalom that if he only killed David, the battle would be over and everyone would unify around him.

Absalom and everyone liked the idea, but God had a different plan. Just to be clear, Ahithophel's advice probably would have meant the death of David and Absalom would rule in his place, but when the Lord has other plans, even the soundest advice will be overruled by foolishness. Fortunately for David, Absalom had received Hushai as an advisor and he was about to bear the fruit David had intended for him.

Hushai began by belittling Ahithophel's advice. He acknowledged that Ahithophel was normally right, just not this time. Hushai then began by appealing to what Absalom knew about his father. He also told the truth, that David probably wouldn't spend the night with the troops, and that they were all fierce warriors, but he also knew that Ahithophel was right about David being tired.

Then Hushai appealed to Absalom's fear by telling him that if one of David's scouts saw his men approaching and started the battle, the men of Israel may grow afraid and scatter and then the battle and kingdom would be lost. Hushai advised Absalom to wait until he could muster the entire army to attack David, something he knew would fail.

Hushai, and all Israel, had watched for years as David's small band of men had conquered kingdoms a hundred times their size. David's only strategic disadvantage at this point was being on the run, something he had not had to do in a very long time. Once he was settled and had time to think, Hushai knew that no one could defeat him.

Absalom fell for Hushai's plot. Because of his close relation to David, Absalom decided to take Hushai's advice. Absalom didn't choose one over the other because one actually sounded better, but because the Lord was confusing Absalom's plans for His own purposes.

God would do the same thing with King Rehoboam in a couple generations. Instead of listening to the sound counsel of the elders of Israel, he instead listened to his young friends. He gave the people a harsh response to the questions they asked him and he turned them away to rebellion with his answer.

> So the king did not listen to the people, for this turn of events was from the Lord, to fulfill the word the Lord had spoken to Jeroboam son of Nebat through Ahijah the Shilonite.
>
> 1 Kings 12:15

Rehoboam didn't do this because it was wise, but because the Lord set him up to fail at this for His own purposes, the same way it was with Hushai and Ahithophel's advice. God did not want Absalom to succeed.

DAVID'S SPIES
17:15-22

Immediately after Hushai realized that Absalom was going to take his advice, he thought it wise to alert David to prepare for what was coming. He told Zadok and Abiathar, the priests still loyal to David, to send word to him about Absalom's plans.

The young men Jonathan and Ahimaaz were waiting in hiding because they knew Absalom would keep his eyes out for them. Israel was a big nation at this point, but not that big, and the group of leaders was an even smaller set of people. We should think of Jerusalem in these days less like Washington D.C. and more like a small town where everyone knows each other.

David's spies were spotted and a chase ensued. They knew that Absalom's pursuers were right on their tail, so as they ran they found a man they knew would give them shelter. In a scene deserving the intensity of a Hollywood blockbuster, they narrowly escaped by hiding in a hand-dug well in the man's courtyard.

The woman who had covered the well and was sitting there guarding it knew better than to tell Absalom's men that she hadn't seen the men. That would give it away that they may be on the premises. Instead, she sent them on a wild goose chase in the wrong direction.

Once the danger had passed, the two men hurried to tell David and all his men to cross the Jordan river before Absalom changed his mind and decided to follow Ahithophel's advice.

AHITHOPHEL'S SUICIDE
17:23

Once Ahithophel realized Absalom had not followed his advice, he knew there was no chance that David would be taken. He knew how this story was going to end, and the fact that he had defected to Absalom's side was not going to go well for him. His bitterness over David's treatment of his family and marriage to Bathsheba had gotten the best of him.

Ahithophel knew that he would be put to death once David returned to Jerusalem, so he decided to end his life on his own terms. When the Bible says that Ahithophel put his house in order, it probably means more than just cleaning it. He probably went and settled any debts, paid all his bills and made sure everything he owned would pass on to his children and grandchildren once he was gone.

Ahithophel was wise, but his bitterness caused him to be at odds with the Lord's will. We are forced on many occasions in our lives to choose sides, so when we do, we should seek the face of the Lord to find out which side He is on. Sometimes He will tell us to choose one over the other, but very often He is on neither side. Asking His opinion can spare us a fate like Ahithophel.

HELP FOR DAVID
17:24-29

When David was alerted to Hushai's plans, he and all his men quickly crossed the Jordan river and headed quickly to the walled city of Mahanaim. Absalom had now mustered the entire army of Israel and he installed another of his relatives as the commander over the army. The exact relation of this relative remains mysterious.

Our author tells us that Amasa was the son of Abigail, the sister of Zeruiah, Joab's mother. Zeruiah was David's sister (or perhaps his sister-in-law), so that makes Amasa his nephew as well. What is peculiar here is the fact that we are told that Abigail was the daughter of Nahash. There is disagreement among scholars as to whether this is the same Nahash that had oppressed Israel at the beginning of Saul's reign. Some even say that Nahash was another name for David's father Jesse. We don't know for sure exactly who we're talking about, but one thing is for sure: Amasa was still part of David's extended family.

This was more than a civil war; it was a bitter rivalry between every part of David's family. A battle was about to begin that was truly brother against brother within David's house. Nathan's prophecy was coming painfully true for David, and it must have been devastating.

But God never stopped loving David. Those God loves, He disciplines.

> *My son, do not despise the Lord's discipline,*
> *and do not resent his rebuke,*
> *because the Lord disciplines those he loves,*
> *as a father the son he delights in.*
>
> *Proverbs 3:11-12*

David was under that discipline, but God still had made provisions for David and his men. When they arrived in Mahanaim, people were there who God had made ready to supply them for the coming battle. When we find ourselves in the midst of hardships, struggles and yes, even literal battles, we can still trust that the Lord still loves us. Even when we are the reason for our own struggles.

The people that lived on the East side of the Jordan River were ready to supply David's troops. They had to leave so quickly, David's small army probably did not have enough food and drink to sustain them for the battle that would more than likely start the next day. This provision was a literal godsend for David and his men, and it gave them strength in the midst of the most emotionally challenging time of David's life.

Don't forget to read 2 Samuel this week!
Visit 10WeekBible.com for more resources including daily podcasts, videos and more.

2 SAMUEL 18-19

STUDY QUESTIONS

1. Why didn't Joab and the men let David go into battle with them?

2. Why would David ask Joab, Abishai and Ittai to be kind to Absalom? Would you have done the same thing?

3. Why do you think Joab killed Absalom instead of arresting him?

4. Why do you think Ahimaaz wanted to tell David about the battle so badly? Why did he lie?

5. Why do you think David wanted Judah, and not all the tribes of Israel to bring him back to Jerusalem?

6. Why did David give Ziba half of Mephibosheth's land instead of taking it all away again?

7. Why do you think David let his men and the people of Judah answer the people from the other tribes of Israel so harshly?

COMMENTARY NOTES

2 SAMUEL CHAPTER 18

GOD SAVE THE KING
18:1-5

In a matter of hours, David had to reestablish his military and organize them based on who he had with him. In the moment, he handed out appointments of generals, colonels, majors and on down the line. David now trusted Ittai, the man who had just arrived a few days before from Gath, with a third of his troops. Sometimes the best leaders are not the people who have been around you for a long time, but the ones who arrive who appear imminently more capable.

David appointed the men in three bands, one to Joab, one to Abishai and one to Ittai. He was going to go out with them to face Absalom, but Joab and the men wouldn't hear of it. We will read later that after an encounter with the Philistines many years earlier, the men decided David could never fight with them again. Again, they wouldn't hear of it here.

David stood at the gate of Mahanaim as all the troops marched out in preparation to meet Absalom and his men. David waited until this very moment to warn Joab and Abishai not to harm Absalom. He knew that if he had told them in private, they would have found some way to kill him and make it look like an accident. He put them on notice in front of all the troops.

David knew Joab all too well, and he had reason not to trust him with this assignment. Unfortunately, the risk of being ratted out to David wasn't enough to keep Joab from doing what he felt was going to be necessary to end this rebellion.

THE DEATH OF ABSALOM
18:6-15

The battle quickly ensued and entered a forest. It is hard to think of there being a forest like this anywhere in this area now, but we know that much of the area was actually forested back then. Thousands of years of deforestation and war has left Israel and Jordan a much more barren landscape than it was then.

The forest was thick, and just as Hushai had known, Israel was no match for David's men when they were rested and prepared. Because the people of Israel knew they had lost the fight, they fled through the woods and our author tells us that the number of people that died accidentally in the forest was greater than those who were killed in battle. Absalom met his end because of the forest, too.

Imagine how painful it must have been for Absalom to hang there in that tree by his hair! He probably wasn't there very long before Joab's men found him. He may have even been unconscious because it seems hard to believe that he wouldn't have cut his hair just to free himself from the tree, but still the soldiers were too afraid to kill him when they found him. They had all heard David's words and were terrified of him.

When the men ran to Joab, he was angry with them. He told them that he would have given them gifts and trophies in front of the rest of the fighting men had they killed Absalom right then and there. But these men were too smart for that. They knew Joab. They knew that if they had killed Absalom, they would have become Joab's scapegoat when David became angry.

Joab's ambition and desire for power and leadership wasn't lost on these men, and he wasn't going to let Absalom threaten his place in the kingdom for another minute. In all of Joab's actions, it is difficult to tell if he was acting in the best interest of Israel or only his own. It seems Israel may have lucked out that Joab's ambitions often coincided with Israel's interests.

Joab took three spears, not one, and thrust each one through Absalom's heart. On seeing that, Joab's ten member guard began hacking Absalom up. It must have been a gruesome sight.

ABSALOM'S MONUMENT
18:16-18

Joab knew that once Absalom was dead, with Israel in flight, that the rebellion would be over. He took his trumpet and blew it in such a way that the army knew to stop their pursuit. Even in Joab's often blind ambition, he was wise enough to know that there had to be a people to rule if he wanted to stay in charge, and nothing good could come of continuing to slaughter their own countrymen.

Joab's men then went and took Absalom's body and gave it the least royal burial possible. He died and was buried with no fanfare, further confirming the word of the Lord through Nathan the prophet. David had said that for the one lamb the rich man in Nathan's story had taken, he should pay back five. By David's own words would his family's judgment be carried out: David would pay for Uriah's death five times over from his children.

Our author tells us that Absalom set up a monument for himself because he had not childrend, but Absalom had children. His daughter he even named after his sister, Tamar. Why Absalom set up a monument for himself, then, is a mystery. Ancient historians believed he set it up in case his children died, but others believe he set it up when he was young because of his young arrogance and conceit. Either way, the monument was telling of how much Absalom thought of himself from a young age.

GOOD NEWS AND BAD NEWS
18:19-33

Ahimaaz, the young man who had come with Hushai's news from Jerusalem, was there with Joab. He wanted to go to David to give him the news that the rebellion had ended. Joab wasn't sure how David was going to react to the news. Joab was standing by twice when messengers brought news they thought was good news to David only to lose their lives. Joab liked Ahimaaz, and knowing that David had a habit of killing the messenger, he had other plans.

There happened to be a Cushite, an African foreigner, that Joab had in mind for the job. Both of the times David had killed the messengers before, they were foreigners. Joab probably thought that if he sent a messenger to deliver the news, it may go better for him when David found out it was him who had killed Absalom. Joab was counting on David killing the Cushite and that killing him would satisfy David's anger. He was greatly mistaken.

Ahimaaz eventually talked Joab into letting him go. It seems like Ahimaaz wanted to be able to put a good spin on the news instead of it being about Absalom. He so wanted to bring David good news that he outran the foreigner and hatched a plan to lie incredibly poorly when he got there.

The watchman on the wall somehow knew it was Ahimaaz coming by the way he ran. How he knew this is a mystery, but maybe people were more keen to perceive things like that instead of what kind of car they drove.

Ahimaaz told David that the battle was over and that they had won. When David asked pointedly about Absalom, Ahimaaz told a bald-faced lie. Ahimaaz's plan didn't work out the way he thought it would because David made him wait to the side until after he had heard the Cushite's message.

When David asked him directly about Absalom, he revelled in what he thought was great news that the king's rebellious son was dead. The way the Cushite gave David the news, it almost seems like Joab had put the worst possible words in his mouth on purpose. It truly seems like Joab was trying to get him killed. Unfortunately for Joab, David wasn't angry.

He was devastated.

David's family had already been broken. Now it was shattered. David lamented loud enough for everyone to hear and wished that he had died instead of Absalom. This may have been one of the lowest moments in David's life, and any parent can probably understand why.

2 SAMUEL CHAPTER 19

MOURNING
19:1-8

David continued his mourning without thinking of the men who had just fought that day in battle. When everyone heard about David's mourning for Absalom, they were too embarrassed to revel in their great and decisive victory.

This enraged Joab. He was afraid that if David didn't change his tune, everyone would sneak away from the city by night and never return to David's side. No doubt Joab had thought about what that would mean for him as commander!

Joab reprimanded David for his behavior. In this moment, he truly did need it because Joab was right. If David didn't rally the men and thank them for their valor, he was going to lose their hearts.

David put himself together and came out and met with the fighting men, which lifted their spirits. Being David's nephew, Joab may have been the only person around who could speak such truth to power in that moment. Regardless of his motives, David needed to hear what Joab was telling him then.

DAVID CALLED BACK TO JERUSALEM
19:9-15

After the people of Israel had time to lick their wounds from the battle, they began to realize how good they had it with David. Some weeks or even months had passed and David was still in Mahanaim, and now a growing contingent of people in Israel wanted to bring David back.

It's not clear why David sent word to Zadok and Abiathar to entice Judah to call him back. It could have been that he was ready to come back to his home, or it could have been because he heard what was being said in Israel and he wasn't ready to forgive them quite yet. David seemed to really want the people of Judah to bring him back into Jerusalem.

In his message to the people of Judah, he also expressed his great anger at Joab. In what seems to be an open letter to Judah, he let them know that he found out it was Joab who had killed Absalom and he had appointed a new commander in his place for when he got back. Judah decided that it was their honor to welcome David back, and they seemed to like the idea of getting first dibs on their rightful king.

GROVELLING
19:16-23

As soon as David and his men reached the Jordan River, an entourage was there to meet him. Shimei, who had cursed David and thrown rocks and dust on him as he left Jerusalem before now came to beg for his life.

We see that Shimei was a wealthy man because he brought people out to help David move all his supplies across the river. He carried weight within the tribe of Benjamin, and as such he arrived to show that he would make sure that Benjamin rallied again around David. He wanted to grovel for David's forgiveness, because he knew that what he had done amounted to treason.

Abishai wasn't satisfied with his contrition and wanted him dead. David didn't trust Shimei either, as we will see when David is on his death bed, but he was not going to execute anyone on a day of celebration. He rebuked Abishai for his bloodthirstiness and gave Shimei an oath that he would not kill him. Take note that David's oath was that *he* would not kill him.

It is interesting to note that Ziba was also with Shimei. David probably found this to be odd, but Ziba knew that David was very soon going to find out the truth: that he had lied to the king about Mephibosheth. Ziba had no way of stopping the truth from coming out, so he was there at the river to beg for his life as well.

Mephibosheth
19:24-30

Mephibosheth quickly came and met King David. Knowing that he didn't have a way to prove what Ziba had said was a lie, he devised a plan to at least show David that Ziba had deceived them both.

Mephibosheth stopped shaving, stopped trimming his toenails and stopped washing his clothes from the day David left until that moment. He wanted some proof that what Ziba had said about him wasn't true, and this was a truly clever way to prove it! Living in his own stench and filth for weeks and months must have been terrible, but it convinced David instantly.

David saw him and was obviously hurt that Mephibosheth hadn't gone with him. Up to this point, David only knew the story Ziba had told him, but when he saw Mephibosheth and heard his story, he was immediately convinced. David had promised everything to Ziba, but now instead of reversing that he had a better plan.

Ziba had betrayed Mephibosheth because he wanted what belonged to him. For years, Ziba had cared for Saul's property as his own, and in a day David gave it all away. Ziba went from owner of a vast fortune to employee in minutes without a second thought from David. Now David realized the error in his judgment and told Mephibosheth and Ziba to divide Saul's estate equally.

David knew that Ziba and Mephibosheth wouldn't trust each other again after this, and he wasn't going to dishonor Ziba for taking care of Saul's estate all these years, even though he lied to the king about Mephibosheth. It almost seems as if David was so tired of dealing with them that he just told them to split everything down the middle and move on with their lives.

The last word of it was when Mephibosheth told David to let Ziba have everything. David never responds, so we do not know if he granted everything to Ziba or if this was Mephibosheth trying to go overboard vowing his loyalty to David.

BARZILLAI
19:31-40

While David and his men had lived in Mahanaim, a wealthy man named Barzillai had provided for them. During Absalom's rebellion, the entire nation had moved to viewing him as their king, so David lost his ability to tax the people for his needs. Even though the rebellion was short-lived, David waited in Mahanaim for a while before returning home. During that time, Barzillai had spent what must have been a fortune feeding, clothing and housing David's men.

Those on the east side of the Jordan river had been all but forgotten during the reign of Saul until his son Ish-Bosheth had decided to take refuge there. It was David who extended the boundaries of Israel to what God had promised to Moses, creating a buffer in the east to protect against raiders coming in and killing entire villages of Israelites.

David spent kingdom money erecting forts and towers to protect the cities of the north and east, so they were immediately loyal when David crossed the Jordan to escape Absalom. Now that David was returning and would have access to his capitol, kingdom and money again he wanted to repay Barzillai by making him someone in the kingdom.

David wanted to provide him with a diplomatic job in Jerusalem, a salary and probably free room and board. Barzillai was old and infirmed, however, and he didn't want to move. He knew that in Jerusalem his life would consist of wonderful food, entertainment and luxury. Barzillai was hard of hearing, probably partly blind and he didn't taste food very well anymore. He was an old man who would rather live out the end of his life in the comfort of his easy chair eating the same thing every day. He had his routine and he didn't want it to change.

As a wealthy businessman he wasn't going to let such an offer from the king go to waste, though. Although it doesn't say it here, many scholars believe that Kimham was Barzillai's son or relative. He asked David that whatever good he was going to do for him he do instead for Kimham.

David was overly gracious to Kimham on account of Barzillai's generosity. David turned Barzillai's request around and said that he would do whatever Barzillai requested for Kimham. Although not in this text, scholars believe that David granted Kimham a town near Bethlehem that was named after him and later referenced in Jeremiah 41:17.

THE RIFT
19:41-43

After David had come back to Jerusalem, the people of Israel quickly came to him to ask why they were left out of the procession to bring David him back. Instead of finding an audience with the king, David only let them speak to his officials.

It seems like David wasn't forgiving of the other ten tribes of Israel giving up on him so quickly, so he let his officials answer the Israelites harshly. David knew how to extend grace in difficult situations, but this seemed a bridge too far for him now. He just couldn't let go of the little bitterness he was holding on to, and it was going to cost him and the nation again.

Because of that bitterness, David and his men sent away the elders of Israel. They felt like second-class citizens now compared to the people of Judah, a foolish thing for David to do to them in the midst of trying to reunify his kingdom.

The civil war wasn't over just yet.

Don't forget to read 2 Samuel this week!
Visit 10WeekBible.com for more resources including daily podcasts, videos and more.

2 SAMUEL 20-22

STUDY QUESTIONS

1. Why did Sheba rebel against David? Why did Israel follow him?

2. Why did David choose to have Amasa chase Sheba instead of Joab?

3. Why did Joab kill Amasa?

4. Why do you think the Lord allowed the Gibeonites to ask for the death of Saul's sons? In what way do you think justice was done by their deaths?

5. What sense do you get about David and his men from reading the account of their battles with the Philistines? Why do you think the author included these specific stories?

6. Why do you think they included this song of David here instead of in the book of Psalms?

7. How do you think David could say that he was blameless before the Lord? How could he say that he was sinless? How can you say the same thing today?

COMMENTARY NOTES

2 SAMUEL CHAPTER 20

THE REBELLION OF SHEBA
20:1-22

After the elders of Israel realized that David and his men were making it clear that they had not yet been forgiven for their rebellion, they went away angry. After all, Judah had been the ones to first anoint and follow Absalom, so they probably felt that David's anger was misplaced.

David was foolish to send them away as he did, and their outrage was justified. No sooner had they left than did an elder from Benjamin rally Israel to another rebellion. As soon as the civil war had ended, David caused it to flare up again.

Sheba the Benjamite rallied all Israel around him now, including those on the east side of the Jordan. It seems like this all was taking place within the day that David had returned to Jerusalem. As soon as David regained his kingdom he lost it again. The tensions were high and David terribly mismanaged the situation.

Before attending to the new rebellion, David had some personal business to attend to. He went to his harem and prepared them for a new life outside the harem. Because Absalom had slept with them, David was never going to again, but he was going to take care of them. He gave them a new house and locked them inside under guard. They were kept in isolation the rest of their lives. As tragic as it was for them, David did not want to risk another rebellion trying to gain ground because someone slept with his concubines.

As soon as he had them locked away, he went to Amasa, his new commander, and had him rally the fighting men of Judah to put down Sheba's rebellion. He gave Amasa three days to get the army together and be back in Jerusalem.

Unfortunately, Amasa wasn't as capable as Joab was at leading the army. For whatever reason, Amasa didn't return within three days. Amasa must not have taken King David's command as seriously as he should have, but David was growing nervous that if Sheba had any more time, he would firmly establish himself against Judah and David.

Since Amasa was still gone, David turned to Abishai (not Joab), and told him to take "his master's" men and chase down Sheba. David was still so angry at Joab he wouldn't utter his name, even in the presence of his brother. Abishai took the men along with David's royal guard and set out to find Sheba.

Before they had gotten far, Amasa found the men and approached them. Amasa found Joab and went up to greet him, probably thinking he would ask Joab for he and his men to join his official army. Amasa must not have been familiar enough with Joab's insatiable appetite for power and control, or he would have been on his guard.

114

As Amasa walked up, Joab dropped his sword into his hand. Amasa took no notice, and before he could finish his greeting of Joab, he had a knife in his stomach. Joab twisted the sword and split Amasa up and down through his mid-section so that when he pulled it out of him, his sword had completely ripped Amasa open and now his innards spilled onto the ground.

Amasa was as gruesome a sight as it sounds. When all the fighting men came to Amasa, they stopped in their tracks to look. Like a horrible train wreck, human nature made every man stop and gape at what had become of Amasa. At that point, someone called all the men to rally around Joab. Now that the men's hearts were with him again, Joab covered up Amasa so no one would see him and stop.

In a moment of bloody rage, Joab had effectively stolen the army back away from David for himself. Immediately, Joab and the men of Judah took off in search for Sheba.

Sheba had been working hard to rally Israel and had found a fortified city to rally around him, exactly what David was afraid of. Joab and the troops settled in for a long battle for Abel Beth Maakah. They began cutting down trees in the area to make a siege ramp.

Many fortified cities had multiple walls so that if one wall was breached, the city would not immediately fall. Abel Beth Maakah apparently had at least two walls. Somehow, Joab and the men of Judah were able to overpower Sheba's army on the outer wall and captured it. Siege ramps were often only one part of the assault on a city, because if you couldn't secure the wall first, it only took one man with burning tar to set the entire siege ramp on fire.

Before they could take the inner wall, Joab's men had to destroy part of the outer wall so they could set up the siege ramp again against the inner wall. There wouldn't have been enough space between the two to build a new one, so part of the wall had to come down.

Again Joab's men cut down trees to build a battering ram and started pounding the wall. Most Westerners think of the castles in Europe when they think of fortified cities, but the fortified cities of the Middle East were far superior to European ones. They were so much better, and had been for millennia, that when the Crusaders invaded the Middle East they were amazed at how well-built the castles there were. It actually dramatically changed European castle-building afterwards.

Abel-Beth Maakah was a powerfully fortified city, and this was no quick battle. Joab and his men had pinned Sheba inside the city, but it was going to take a lot or time to get him out. It wasn't until a wise woman inside the city realized that it was just a matter of time before Joab would breach both walls and kill anyone inside they thought was harboring Sheba.

She probably knew that Joab was going to kill the entire city to strike fear into Israel so that no one else would try to rebel, so she convinced the locals to give up Sheba and his men. After a short exchange with Joab from atop the wall (possibly at night to prevent Sheba's men from killing her for her insolence), a truce was agreed upon.

Abel Beth Maakah would be spared for the price of Sheba's head being tossed over the wall, which was produced in short order. True to his word, Joab left the city alone as soon as he had the rebel leader's head in hand to show to David.

THE NEW ARMY
20:23-26

When Joab showed back up in Jerusalem with the head of Sheba, David probably had a thousand questions. By now, he certainly had heard that Joab had killed Amasa in cold blood. David probably wasn't too broken up about that since Amasa had cost them so much time that Sheba had time to find a fortified city to call his capitol.

But David hated Joab. He was angry at him for killing Abner in cold blood. Now he was angry at Joab for killing Amasa in cold blood, but the worst thing of all was that Joab killed Absalom. Joab hadn't committed murder with that act since they were at war with each other, but David couldn't forgive Joab for killing Absalom. He had specifically told him not to and because of Joab's ambitions to lead the army he killed him anyway.

At this point, David had tried to remove Joab three times. It seems like David had just given up on trying to keep his nephew out of leadership. David wouldn't put him to death on account of his sister, and it seems like David realized it would be far less bloody for anyone who would be foolish enough to get in Joab's way. So David just let Joab run the military from then on. And it would stay that way until David uttered his last words to Solomon.

> *"Now you yourself know what Joab son of Zeruiah did to me—what he did to the two commanders of Israel's armies, Abner son of Ner and Amasa son of Jether. He killed them, shedding their blood in peacetime as if in battle, and with that blood he stained the belt around his waist and the sandals on his feet. Deal with him according to your wisdom, but do not let his gray head go down to the grave in peace.*

> *1 Kings 2:5-6*

At the end of our chapter we learn a new name: Benaiah son of Jehoiada. He will be David's answer to Joab for Solomon.

2 SAMUEL CHAPTER 21

THE GIBEONITES
21:1-14

This is one of the hardest passages in the Old Testament to deal with, but it will give us an opportunity to learn from the Lord something important. The Lord takes oaths very seriously, and He takes the cries of oppressed people even more seriously.

When the seasonal rains didn't come the third year in a row, David knew something was wrong, so he sought the Lord. The Lord spoke to David and told him that the famine in the land was because of the actions of Saul when he killed the Gibeonites. This must have shocked David on multiple levels.

First of all, why was God just now getting around to judging the nation for something that happened decades in the past? Second, why was God judging Israel under David's leadership for something Saul did? Third, what was David supposed to do to fix it? Our author doesn't tell us that God gave David any direction to solve the problem.

Maybe not immediately, but at some point quickly David realized what was going on. He knew that God doesn't only hear the prayers of Israelites, but the prayers of anyone who cries out to Him. David understood that the Gibeonites had been crying out to the Lord for a generation, and God couldn't hold his anger in anymore.

God is a God of justice, and it is when people have been wronged God gets angry. He gets angry on their behalf. The Gibeonites had been asking the Lord to avenge them because they were now powerless to do it themselves.

This all started with a lie they told to Joshua when the Israelites were taking the land hundreds of years before. They told Joshua they were from a distant land when in fact they were from a town directly in the sights of Israel's army. The whole story is found in Joshua 9, but what is important is that Joshua swore an oath to the Gibeonites that they would not be killed when the Israelites took the land.

Three days after they made the treaty with the

Gibeonites, the Israelites heard that they were neighbors, living near them. So the Israelites set out and on the third day came to their cities: Gibeon, Kephirah, Beeroth and Kiriath Jearim. But the Israelites did not attack them, because the leaders of the assembly had sworn an oath to them by the Lord, the God of Israel.

> *The whole assembly grumbled against the leaders, but all the leaders answered, "We have given them our oath by the Lord, the God of Israel, and we cannot touch them now. This is what we will do to them: We will let them live, so that God's wrath will not fall on us for breaking the oath we swore to them." They continued, "Let them live, but let them be woodcutters and water carriers in the service of the whole assembly." So the leaders' promise to them was kept.*
>
> *Joshua 9:16-21*

The key phrase here is that because of Joshua's foolish promise, he prophesied that God's wrath would fall on the Israelites now if they harmed the Gibeonites. That is exactly what happened when Saul set about killing the foreigners who lived in his hometown area. Saul, and possibly his entire family, had partaken in genocide against the Gibeonites and now few of them were left.

David knew that the Israelites were under God's wrath because the Gibeonites were crying out, so he went to them and asked them what it would take to appease them. They asked for something very hard, but David knew he had to give it to them to appease the Lord's wrath on their behalf.

David gave them seven of Saul's descendants to be killed and their bodies displayed, but not Jonathan's son Mephibosheth. After they had been executed for the genocide of the Gibeonites, God relented of His anger against Saul and Israel.

What makes this passage difficult is that it seems like these seven men were executed for no cause. We must realize that if God saw fit to see these men executed, they must have also born guilt in the matter, even though our author does not explicitly tell us that. When we read that God was angry at "Saul" for his bloodshed, we must read that God is angry at the "house of Saul," his family, for what happened. God gives us the impression that Saul did not act alone in the massacre that took place a generation before.

PHILISTINES
21:15-22

Samuel has been chronological throughout the entire narrative up until now. Starting with this passage, things seem to begin to be summarized over the course of David's career. The stories of the battles with the Philistines seem to fit better with David's earlier conquest as the newly crowned king in Hebron.

These stories specifically tell the stories of the death of Goliath's four brothers (or close relatives), who were all giants. They take place over a period of years and highlight the kind of men David had in his company.

2 SAMUEL CHAPTER 22

DAVID'S SONG
22:1-51

This song is a very poetic expression by David of God's continuing salvation of his life. David was spared from death over and over again throughout his life. Starting with Saul all the way to Abishai's rescue of him from the hands of Goliath's brother, God watched out for David.

One of the most amazing statements of this song is this passage:

"The Lord has dealt with me according to my righteousness;

according to the cleanness of my hands he has rewarded me.

For I have kept the ways of the Lord;

I am not guilty of turning from my God.

All his laws are before me;

I have not turned away from his decrees.

I have been blameless before him

and have kept myself from sin.

The Lord has rewarded me according to my righteousness,

according to my cleanness

"To the faithful you show yourself faithful,

to the blameless you show yourself blameless,

to the pure you show yourself pure,

but to the devious you show yourself shrewd.

You save the humble,

but your eyes are on the haughty to bring them low.

You, Lord, are my lamp;

the Lord turns my darkness into light.

2 Samuel 22:21-29

Our author knows what he has already included in this book about David. Many biographers write only the glowing successes of their subjects, but in Samuel, many of David's greatest moral, spiritual and leadership failures are on display beside his greatness. This passage seems to stand in stark contrast to that reality.

Was David obtusely ignorant of his own sin? Was he lying? Did he choose to overlook his many indiscretions? Or was it that David believed God when He said that He will put our sins as far as the East is from the West.

as far as the east is from the west,

so far has he removed our transgressions from us.

Psalm 103:12

David authored that Psalm, so this was an ever-present reality for him. David knew what he had done. He wasn't stupid and he wasn't demented, but he was rare. He was able to actually see himself through God's eyes: forgiven. That is one of the hardest things for humans to do. It is hard to forgive others who wrong us, but harder still is for us to forgive ourselves from the wrong we do to others.

David believed that God forgave and truly forgot; something people are incredibly bad at. He believed it so well that he wrote this passage here in 2 Samuel 22. He saw himself as clean. David knew that he was pure before God. David's repentance made him clean because God is faithful and just to forgive our sins.

If we confess our sins, he is faithful and just and will forgive us our sins and purify us from all unrighteousness.

1 John 1:9

David knew this inside and out. It is something we could learn well from David. He was so sure of this reality, he actually lived like it. David didn't have to look in the mirror every day and say his affirmations to overcome the doubt he had of this truth. No, David knew God had forgiven him and so he saw himself in every way as clean and righteous: completely free from sin.

If we learn nothing else from David, we need to learn this well.

Don't forget to read 2 Samuel this week!
Visit 10WeekBible.com for more resources including daily podcasts, videos and more.

2 SAMUEL 23-24

STUDY QUESTIONS

1. Why did David reiterate his sinlessness in his last words? How can we make David's understanding of forgiveness as real in our lives as it was to him?

2. Is it okay for David to curse those who were against him like he did in his last words? In what ways should we and shouldn't we do the same thing today?

3. Why do you think David's mighty men organized into the groups that they did?

4. Why do you think God wanted to judge Israel? Does God still do that with nations today?

5. What was David's sin in taking a census? In what way was David's sin related to God's anger and judgment over the nation of Israel?

6. Why did David choose the option of judgment he did? What would you have chosen?

7. Why did God stop the angel of death when He did?

8. What sits on the spot of Araunah's threshing floor today and why is that important?

COMMENTARY NOTES

2 SAMUEL CHAPTER 23

DAVID'S LAST WORDS
23:1-7

David saw his words as inspired. He knew that what he was writing was from God. David is acknowledging that these words were as anointed as Moses' and Abraham's. What an amazing reality and a heavy burden! David knew who he was and took that role with gladness and sobriety.

David reminded everyone that he was the hero of their songs. He was the one who killed Goliath and had the women of Israel sing that he was their champion here. He was the one God Himself chose to anoint as king in the place of wicked Saul. This same David is the one who is going to utter this inspired word now.

What is that word? That he was a righteous ruler. That God's favor was on Israel because of him and his leadership over the nation. That Israel had conquered all the land promised to Moses because of David. Was it arrogant for David to say such things? Was it wrong? This seems less like Holy Spirit inspired writing and the words of an arrogant, self-absorbed narcissist.

But that is not what this is. That isn't who David was. This was truly inspired and our author includes it immediately following David's song so we can further understand David's amazing relationship to God that we need to emulate.

David's righteousness didn't come from his lack of sin, but rather God's ability to forgive and forget that sin. David knew that he was a righteous ruler because He sought God's face in everything he did and when he screwed it up he sought God's forgiveness. Righteousness, even in the Old Testament, did not come from one's ability to follow the Law, but from one's faith in God to forgive. Paul spends considerable time explaining this concept in the book of Romans.

The problem is that having faith in God to forgive is not natural. It's hard. We would much rather trust in our own ability to make things right than to just trust and hope that God is nice and will forgive us. Even though it's a lot harder in reality (impossible, really), it normally feels easier to try and earn our favor back with God when we sin. The more we try to earn that favor back, the emptier we become and we actually end up sinning all the more.

David knew the solution to this. As a leader, any leader, you're going to have a lot more opportunity to sin against others. Most people aren't constantly asked to make life and death decisions or to adjudicate between others. Leaders, depending on their capacity and position, do it often. If you can't have faith in the Lord to forgive you when you mess up and repent and to help fix the negative situations you cause, you will actually end up causing a lot more harm in the end.

There were a lot of things David couldn't fix, but he

trusted the Lord to do it. That is what a righteous leader was and that's how David could have confidence that he was one. David tells us that he knows he was right with God and that is why God made a covenant with Him that the Messiah would come from his family.

David finishes his last words by saying that evil men will be dealt with; that they will receive judgment. He seems to be specifically calling out those who intentionally lie to defame others or to gain an upper hand as "wicked men." David was all too familiar with this. Think about how politics and Washington, D.C. work today. It's like the old political adage, "How do you know when a politician is lying? When they open their mouth."

Lying is incredibly expedient when trying to gain something quickly or to try and destroy and dismantle political opponents. The last of David's last words are to say that these liars are like thorns that are dealt with using hot and sharp tools of iron. His final words are those of judgment.

David understood, and wanted to convey with his last words, that it is the position of the heart, not of the mouth or actions, that determine a person's righteousness. What a wonderful New Testament theology explained to us right in the middle of the Old Testament!

ISRAEL'S MIGHTY MEN
23:8-39

As we read through these passages about David's mighty men, we discover that there was a hierarchy that must have developed somewhat naturally. It probably started in the days when David was in the cave of Adullam and the misfits of Israel gathered to him. In those days the men began to separate and distinguish themselves through their actions.

The men loved David and served him faithfully even when he probably didn't deserve their loyalty. As we have looked at David's life, one thing sets him apart and it makes it clear why he would have been a man these mighty men would have followed: his character.

Even the bravest of leaders often melt when faced with difficult decisions and situations. David never did. He was the young man who ran *toward* Goliath when all Israel cowered. His confidence in God's love, learned from singing to the Lord as a youth, gave him uncommon confidence in himself in ways that were different from others. The stories here are of men who would not follow just anyone. Their presence lends further credence to the character of David.

The organization of them that naturally evolved was that there was a leader among them all: Joab. Under Joab were "the three:" Josheb-Basshebeth, the greatest of the three, Eleazar and Shammah. Abishai wasn't considered one of them but was their commander. Next came "the thirty." Benaiah was just as famous among the men as Abishai, Joab and "the three," but he wasn't one of them. He would go on to be Solomon's commander.

"The three" and "the thirty" were probably the nicknames David's men gave to themselves. Abishai and Benaiah couldn't be considered one of them not because they weren't worthy, but because they were the terms of endearment of the men at the time who did amazing exploits. It's like the "Rat Pack," although there were many other good singers in Frank Sinatra's day, no one will ever be added to their exclusive group (if you don't know what that is, Google it).

The exploits that our author tells us here are amazing. These feats of strength in war are the stuff of legend, and everyone in Israel had heard them. They were as famous in Israel as you can imagine they would be. But more important than that, they are now famous for eternity.

When these men arrived at the cave of Addulam, they were running away from people they owed money to. They were sick of their bosses. Some wanted to overthrow Saul in an assassination attempt. None of them were exactly the kind of people you want fighting on behalf of your nation. But along the way, David sat with them. He sang with them. He fought with them. He ate with them.

David was not only their military leader, he was their spiritual discipler. He taught them how to live and walk before the Lord. They saw David, in the moment when they wanted to stone him, "strengthen himself in God" (1 Samuel 30:6). He took a rag-tag bunch of outcasts and turned them into Israel's

Mighty Men.

One final sad note in this chapter is the fact that Uriah the Hittite was one of the thirty. He had surely been there since the cave and had been faithful to David all his years until his death. His only crime was having a beautiful wife.

The amazing thing about this chapter is that it begins with David's assurance that he is righteous and pure, free from sin, and ends with the name of one of his greatest sins. David truly knew how to live within the grace of the Lord, and he did it a thousand years before Jesus made that grace as clear as we know it today. Oh, that we could live with that kind of assurance in God's love and grace today that David did then!

2 SAMUEL CHAPTER 24

THE CENSUS
24:1-9

This chapter is an interesting way to end 2 Samuel, but it has an important point to it. This census wasn't inspired by David, but by God. If the fact that God was angry so He inspired David to sin isn't strange enough, the same story in 1 Chronicles gives us a little different picture that raises even more questions.

Satan rose up against Israel and incited David to take a census of Israel.

1 Chronicles 21:1

The author of Chronicles tells us that it was actually Satan who caused David to sin. So, which was it? Was it God, or was it Satan?

The Short answer is both.

Much like the story of Job, God was really the one who needed Job to go through a time of testing. God used the willing volunteer He had in Satan to carry that out. God never tempts men to sin, but He always has the same volunteer willing to step in. In the end, however, God always uses the tragedy of sin and judgment for our good.

God was angry with the Israelites for their sin. The "again" seems like a reference to the anger of the Lord against Israel on behalf of the Gibeonites. So what was Israel's sin this time? We are not told, but the manner with which God chose to judge Israel is of some insight.

> Then the Lord said to Moses, "When you take a census of the Israelites to count them, each one must pay the Lord a ransom for his life at the time he is counted. Then no plague will come on them when you number them. Each one who crosses over to those already counted is to give a half shekel, according to the sanctuary shekel, which weighs twenty gerahs. This half shekel is an offering to the Lord. All who cross over, those twenty years old or more, are to give an offering to the Lord. The rich are not to give more than a half shekel and the poor are not to give less when you make the offering to the Lord to atone for your lives. Receive the atonement money from the Israelites and use it for the service of

*the tent of meeting. It will be a memorial for the
Israelites before the Lord, making atonement for
your lives."*

Exodus 30:11-16

It is very interesting that the Lord incited David to count the men but not pay the ransom. This offering was to atone for the people's sin, and the Lord wanted whatever sin was going on in Israel equated with that. The money was supposed to be used to make provisions for the tabernacle, and again, the Lord wanted this event equated with that as you will see by the end of the chapter.

In the end, we are not told what the sin was, but we will see where the Lord is going with this. The fact that even Joab saw that this was a bad idea is telling as to how divine this entire affair was. The Lord was not judging Israel because of David's sin in taking the census, He was already angry before the census. He wanted Israel to understand that their sin and judgment were related to what was to be atoned for in the census.

THE REVELATION
24:10-14

It took Joab over nine months to take the census, and it wasn't until he was done that David immediately realized what an evil thing it was to take a census. He repented and asked the Lord for forgiveness. That is when Gad received the word of the Lord and came to David.

The fact that we know that God was the one initially angry, and that Satan was allowed to entice David into this new sin means that some sort of prophetic revelation of the matter eventually came to the attention of David and our author.

Gad told David that the Lord was giving him three choices, to which David rightly responded with anxiety. The fact that the three choices were all bad and that David was the one who had to choose which way the Israelites would die must have been a heavy burden. David was having a bad day to say the least, but he was the exact right person for this job, and the Lord wanted him to know that.

Two of the three options had to do with foreign oppressors, one option did not. Through his years, David had learned not to place too much trust in man, but to trust the Lord implicitly. He chose the option that had nothing to do with other men because David was going to do everything in his power to beg God to change His mind, and it was going to work.

THE PLAGUE
24:15-17

David's wisdom was going to prove a great salvation, even though the outcome was still devastating. In a matter of three days seventy thousand people were dead, but the angel in charge of the plague wasn't done yet when he came to Jerusalem. When the Lord told the angel to stop, an amazing thing happened.

At that same time that the Lord told the angel of

death to stop, David was gazing out over Jerusalem interceding. He was crying out to stop and to bring judgment on him instead of Israel. That's when he saw the angel come to a stop at a man's threshing floor atop a hill adjacent to his palace.

The Lord wanted this plague connected with what He was going to place on that hill.

THE ALTAR
24:18-25

Even though David had conquered the city and taken it from the Jebusites, some had obviously been allowed to live and continue to own property. The threshing floor where the angel came to a stop belonged to Araunah the Jebusite.

One of David's prophets came to him with the word of the Lord to build an altar where he had been allowed to see the angel come to stop the plague. As David approached, Araunah must have been terrified. To see the royal entourage come to visit you, one of the foreigners who had previously occupied the city, must have been intimidating.

Araunah asked why David was there, thinking it was to kill or imprison him. He had probably been long expecting this day since he was still hanging around. Instead of death, David came offering money. He was so happy that he wasn't there to lop off his head, Araunah just offered to give the land to David.

David refused to have it for free and paid the market rate for it. He bought two of the oxen Araunah had and sacrificed them there on the altar that was hastily built. After the sacrifice was offered, the plague ended, and that is how our book ends.

But why did God want an altar there? Why did God show David the angel? Why did God cause David to call the census to judge the nation? As we read, when a census was taken, money was supposed to be offered to redeem each man's life that was counted. It was that life ransom that the Lord wanted to highlight.

Even though we are not explicitly told this, we can possibly infer from this that the Lord was angry with the Israelites because they were not faithfully offering the sacrifices He had commanded to atone for their sin. Again, we don't know that for sure, but it is intriguing that God had the plague end on the very plot of ground He would have David buy to put the temple on in Solomon's lifetime.

It was this temple that was the place where atonement was going to be offered for the Israelites for generations, and it was this temple where the veil would eventually be torn in two. David had found the city the Lord had promised His Name would eventually rest upon, and God had shown David the place within that city where the footstool of His glory would rest.

Even though God brought painful judgment on the nation for their sin, He used that tragic moment for their good.

> And we know that in all things God works for
> the good of those who love him, who have been
> called according to his purpose.
>
> Romans 8:28

Our story ends here with God choosing the place where His Name would rest. This plot of ground is the most hotly contested place on planet earth today, and it was established there as the angel of death was stopped. How appropriate that it was this place where the bleakness of everlasting death would end for so many Israelites, and where an everlasting peace through Jesus would be revealed one day.

That same death that was stopped by David's sacrifice that day is like the death that now ends because of the sacrifice of Jesus. How fitting to end this book with the happy thought of death coming to an end, which the Lord has promised us through the life, sacrifice and resurrection of Jesus. It was on this mountain that Isaiah prophesied this:

> *On this mountain the Lord Almighty will prepare*
> *a feast of rich food for all peoples,*
> *a banquet of aged wine—*
> *the best of meats and the finest of wines.*
> *On this mountain he will destroy*
> *the shroud that enfolds all peoples,*
> *the sheet that covers all nations;*
> *he will swallow up death forever.*
> *The Sovereign Lord will wipe away the tears*
> *from all faces;*
> *he will remove his people's disgrace*
> *from all the earth.*
> *The Lord has spoken.*

Isaiah 25:6-8

Thank goodness that the Lord has spoken! He has taken away our disgrace and will wipe the tears away from our eyes. Salvation through the shed blood of Jesus is our greatest joy, comfort and hope.

David looked forward to the day that we now enjoy: salvation through the coming Messiah.

Don't forget to read 2 Samuel this week!
Visit 10WeekBible.com for more resources including daily podcasts, videos and more.

READING CHART

WEEK 1
□ Day 1: Chapters 1-4
□ Day 2: Chapters 5-8
□ Day 3: Chapters 9-12
□ Day 4: Chapters 13-16
□ Day 5: Chapters 17-20
□ Day 6: Chapters 21-24

WEEK 2
□ Day 1: Chapters 1-4
□ Day 2: Chapters 5-8
□ Day 3: Chapters 9-12
□ Day 4: Chapters 13-16
□ Day 5: Chapters 17-20
□ Day 6: Chapters 21-24

WEEK 3
□ Day 1: Chapters 1-4
□ Day 2: Chapters 5-8
□ Day 3: Chapters 9-12
□ Day 4: Chapters 13-16
□ Day 5: Chapters 17-20
□ Day 6: Chapters 21-24

WEEK 4
□ Day 1: Chapters 1-4
□ Day 2: Chapters 5-8
□ Day 3: Chapters 9-12
□ Day 4: Chapters 13-16
□ Day 5: Chapters 17-20
□ Day 6: Chapters 21-24

WEEK 5
□ Day 1: Chapters 1-4
□ Day 2: Chapters 5-8
□ Day 3: Chapters 9-12
□ Day 4: Chapters 13-16
□ Day 5: Chapters 17-20
□ Day 6: Chapters 21-24

WEEK 6
□ Day 1: Chapters 1-4
□ Day 2: Chapters 5-8
□ Day 3: Chapters 9-12
□ Day 4: Chapters 13-16
□ Day 5: Chapters 17-20
□ Day 6: Chapters 21-24

WEEK 7
□ Day 1: Chapters 1-4
□ Day 2: Chapters 5-8
□ Day 3: Chapters 9-12
□ Day 4: Chapters 13-16
□ Day 5: Chapters 17-20
□ Day 6: Chapters 21-24

WEEK 8
□ Day 1: Chapters 1-4
□ Day 2: Chapters 5-8
□ Day 3: Chapters 9-12
□ Day 4: Chapters 13-16
□ Day 5: Chapters 17-20
□ Day 6: Chapters 21-24

WEEK 9
□ Day 1: Chapters 1-4
□ Day 2: Chapters 5-8
□ Day 3: Chapters 9-12
□ Day 4: Chapters 13-16
□ Day 5: Chapters 17-20
□ Day 6: Chapters 21-24

WEEK 10
□ Day 1: Chapters 1-4
□ Day 2: Chapters 5-8
□ Day 3: Chapters 9-12
□ Day 4: Chapters 13-16
□ Day 5: Chapters 17-20
□ Day 6: Chapters 21-24

ABOUT THE AUTHOR

Darren Hibbs is the founder of the 10 Week Bible Study. He believes that the methodology of studying the Bible in this book can radically transform your life with God.

By filling your heart and mind with the Word of God first and foremost, you will better know God's heart than if your Bible knowledge comes primarily from sermons or even the commentary provided within this book. There is nothing more powerful for transformation than a people who know for themselves the Word of God.

Darren's heart burns to bring a message of hope to a lost and broken world through the immeasurable love of Jesus. It is his heart that the church will grow in love for God and embrace His love and power so that the lost will see and hear the good news about Jesus as they see it change us.

Darren writes regularly and can be reached at
www.DarrenHibbs.com.

Other Titles by 10 Week Bible

Titles in Print & Digital Formats:
1 Samuel
2 Samuel
Esther
Daniel
John
Acts
Romans
Revelation

For a full and up-to-date list of titles in print, as well as for bookstore ordering information, visit 10WeekBible.com

Find out more at 10WeekBible.com

10 Week Bible Study Podcast

If you have enjoyed this study, you may also enjoy the 10 Week Bible Study Podcast. This is a five day a week broadcast designed to help you get through each book of the Bible ten weeks at a time. It includes the reading of the entire book being studied once and helpful commentary to encourage your personal reading and study of God's Word.

You can listen to the podcast on any platform on the go or at home. For a list of easy links to subscribe to the podcast, visit 10WeekBible.com.

There, you can also subscribe to the broadcast on You-Tube.

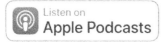

Watch on

Join our group at

Made in United States
Orlando, FL
08 November 2024

53620400R00088